Gerard Manley Hopkins and the Spell of John Duns Scotus

To Margaret

Gerard Manley Hopkins and the Spell of John Duns Scotus

JOHN LLEWELYN

EDINBURGH
University Press

© John Llewelyn, 2015, 2021

Edinburgh University Press Ltd
The Tun - Holyrood Road
12(2f) Jackson's Entry
Edinburgh EH8 8PJ
www.euppublishing.com

First published in hardback by Edinburgh University Press 2015

Typeset in 11/13pt Monotype Ehrhardt by
Servis Filmsetting Ltd, Stockport, Cheshire

A CIP record for this book is available from the British Library

ISBN 978 1 4744 0894 3 (hardback)
ISBN 978 1 4744 6460 4 (paperback)
ISBN 978 1 4744 0895 0 (webready PDF)
ISBN 978 1 4744 0896 7 (epub)

The right of John Llewelyn to be identified as the author of this work has been asserted in accordance with the Copyright, Designs and Patents Act 1988, and the Copyright and Related Rights Regulations 2003 (SI No. 2498).

Contents

Acknowledgements	vi

Part I

1	The Crux	3
2	Instress Scaped and Inscape Stressed	10
3	Parsing the Poem of Parmenides	19
4	Hopkins' Double Discovery, of Scotus and of Himself	30
5	Some Transcendentals	43
6	Another Transcendental?	54

Part II

7	Seeming, Observing and Observance	69
8	Peirce's Post-Kantian Categories	79
9	Ecceity, Ipseity and Existents	90
10	Being as Doing	99
11	From Method of Ignorance to Way of Love	108
12	Categories and Transcendentals Transcended	117

Afterword	127
Notes	132
Selective Bibliography	143
Index	147

Acknowledgements

Approximately a quarter of Chapter 11 is adapted with kind permission from my 'Educated Ignorance', in Gavin Morrison and Sigrid Sandström (eds), *Ignorance: Between Knowing and Not Knowing* (Stockholm: Axl Books, 2015). I thank Channel 4, the estate of Dennis Potter and Faber & Faber for permission to cite the sentences from Dennis Potter reproduced in Chapter 2. The sentences cited in Chapter 7 from *The Peregrine, The Hill of Summer & Diaries* are reprinted by permission of HarperCollins Publishers Ltd ©1967, 1969, 2010, J. A. Baker. For permission to use on the cover of this book a photograph of the sculpture at Duns by Frank Tritschler representing Scotus I thank the Franciscan Order, which commissioned the effigy to mark the seventh centenary of the philosopher's birth. I am especially grateful to Fr Boniface Kruger, OFM, and to Andrew Tulloch of the Scottish Borders Council for helping me toward an answer to the question whether Frank Tritschler is still living. For the photograph of the bust of Scotus on the cover I am indebted to Colin Brydon. For permission to use on the cover a photograph of the sculpture at Regis University, Denver, Colorado, representing Hopkins I thank the sculptor Rowan Gillespie. He suggested I get in touch with Professor Victoria MaCabe of that university. I am indebted to her for broadening the field of photographs from which to choose. I thank all those at or associated with Edinburgh University Press who have cooperated in the production of my study, in particular Carol Macdonald, James Dale, Rebecca Mackenzie, Holly Roberts and Anthony Mercer. I am grateful to the staff of the National Library of Scotland, of the libraries of the University of Edinburgh and of New College on the Mound for their assistance. For the encouragement conveyed by their interest in my endeavour notwithstanding in some cases our disagreement over some of its presuppositions, I

Acknowledgements

thank Gareth Davies, Percy Jack, Donald Maciver, Basil O'Neill, Adriaan Peperzak and certain other generously supportive good friends who in the arcane conventions of book publication are supposed to remain unpublic and unthanked. For hauling me out of technological quagmires or the slough of despondent morale I am indebted to my brothers David and Howard, to my nephews Simon and Steven, and to the Morningside Caffè Nero.

With gratitude for her sustained and sustaining dedication to me, I dedicate this book to my wife Margaret who, birdwatcher like Hopkins and wordwatcher like him and Duns Scotus, is proof of their teaching that loveliness is a noun with a verb at its heart dancing like she does in mine.

What becomes of my verses I care little, but about things like this, what I write or could write on philosophical matters, I do; and the reason of the difference is that the verses stand or fall by their simple selves and, though being read they might do good, by being unread they do no harm; but if the other things are unsaid right they will be said by somebody else wrong, and that is what will not let me rest.

> Gerard Manley Hopkins
> writing to Richard Watson Dixon
> from Dublin
> 27 January 1887

Yet ah! this air I gather and release
He lived on; these weeds and waters, these walls are what
He haunted who of all men most sways my spirit to peace

> Gerard Manley Hopkins
> in 'Duns Scotus's Oxford'
> composed at Oxford
> March 1879

Part I

1
The Crux

The Franciscan friar called, after his place of birth in Scotland, John Duns Scotus (1266–1308) was also called the subtle doctor, *doctor subtilis*. The English Jesuit priest, poet and honorary Welshman Gerard Manley Hopkins (1844–89) called him 'Of realty the rarest-veinèd unraveller.' But unravelling itself calls for unravelling. When nowadays someone says 'Then everything began to unravel' the intention appears to be to say that things then began to fall into a state of confusion. Likewise, when Shakespeare writes of sleep that it 'knits up the ravelled sleeve of care' his meaning seems to be that a state of confusion or entanglement of threads is tidied up. But when in a journal entry for February 1870 Hopkins writes of 'sunlight fallen through ravelled cloud', does he mean that the cloud is entangled, so that the unravelling of it would signify its becoming untangled? That he does mean this is likely, but not obvious. A trace of ambiguity survives. This ambiguity hardens into a contradiction when the *Concise Oxford Dictionary* gives 'entangle' as the first meaning of 'ravel', cites as illustrations 'the ravelled skein of life' and 'fray (intransitive and transitive)', then gives 'disentangle, unravel . . .'. This ambiguity or contradiction may be resolved for a given occasion by checking the context of the text in question. Doing this restores a degree of order in so far as it reveals that the difference between the two meanings corresponds to the difference between transitive and intransitive uses of the verb 'to unravel'. A clue to the meaning Hopkins intends is his distinction between 'the scattered' and 'the ravelled' made in his letter of 24 March 1885 to Robert Bridges. He writes of one of Shakespeare's History plays that there may be many references to matters alluded to in it which are not integrated into the main story being told and which the uninitiated may therefore 'want you to unravel and to gather up'.[1] I shall presume that this is a reliable guide to the sense in which Scotus is for Hopkins 'Of realty the rarest-veinèd unraveller'. This does not exclude the possibility that among the gifts which made Scotus an exceptionally good unraveller according to Hopkins was that of having a fine ear for antilogisms like the pair 'unravel' and 'ravel'.

Such antilogisms could be called Abelian words after Karl Abel, who collected and classified words that admit of being taken in opposite senses.[2] This internal oppositeness of sense of the English word 'ravel' is anticipated by the Dutch word *rafelen*. Yet, as if to make the outrageous suggestion that opposition may be a sort of apposition, in modern English–Dutch dictionaries *rafelen* is given as a translation of the English 'unravel'! Double Dutch. *Lingua subtilis*.

The duplicity just described is exemplified again by some of the words, in particular the words 'inscape' and 'instress', that are cited from Hopkins and analysed in the second chapter of this book. To use another word of which Hopkins is fond, readers may find themselves 'baffled'. They will have tasted the obscurity that Dylan Thomas said he was fascinated by in the poetry of Hopkins. Anticipating the perplexity of those readers, I hereby promise them that by the end of the fourth chapter much of that opacity will be replaced by enlightenment thanks to a demonstration that Hopkins' distinction between inscape and instress is supportable retrospectively by the ingenious distinction Scotus names *distinctio formalis*.

Few poets are as boldly creative with or of words as is Hopkins. He regards it as one of his responsibilities as a poet to make something strange either in the sense of creating something that is strange or in the sense of causing something to become strange. His production of strangeness by neologism and semantic surprise will be the first object of attention in the chapters that follow. Attention will also be directed at his syntactic inventions. Attention to them will lead us to focus attention on attention as such. To elucidate the strange logic and rhetorology of attention in its opposition-apposition with intention is the primary purpose of this book. The fulfilment of that purpose will assist and be assisted by a meditation on the paradoxes of individuality, suchness itself and selfhood as these are provoked by Hopkins' astonishing reading of Scotus and in the works of other philosophers who have fallen under his spell: Charles Sanders Peirce, Martin Heidegger, Hannah Arendt, Jacques Derrida and, cursorily, Ockham, Leibniz, Hume and, still more cursorily, Scotus' other compatriot Thomas Reid and that more recent reader, Gilles Deleuze, who fell under Scotus' spell though without being bound by it.

This book is what the thirteenth-century Franciscan theologian Peter John Olivi would have called an *experimentum suitatis*, a test of the he-ity, she-ity or it-ity that to each one of us individually would present itself as a test of me-ity and what would present itself to the individual Gerard Manley Hopkins as an attestation of what he refers to as his self-taste.

Veritative testing becomes judicative attestation when the me-ity of that self-gusto or self-disgust is accompanied, as it was also for Job, by the before-God, the *coram Deo*. The paradoxes of individuality and suchness referred to above and passim in the following pages taint the -ity of De-ity and the *-itas* of *Divinitas*. They infect the grammar of the G-word under which alone individuality and existence are one with essence. The G-word, and what I provisionally and no doubt irritatingly call the b-word, are two words (unless they turn out to be one and the same word) that play crucial roles in the writings of Hopkins and Scotus. They raise their own particular difficulties. They will therefore receive our close attention in due course.[3] Two complex notions, that of the middle voice or something like it and that of chiasmus, are so crucial for the more exploratory as distinguished from more expository missions of this volume that they call for preliminary attention to be given to them forthwith.

Wittgenstein asks us to imagine a boy who racks his brains over the question whether the verb 'to sleep' means something active or passive.[4] Perhaps the lad is supposing that a verb, or at least a transitive verb, always stands for an action, except that it stands for a passion when it is formulated in the passive voice in order to say that something is or was or will be done to the bearer of the grammatical subject of the verb. But the grammatical labels do not always correspond with the facts on the basis of which we suppose they get attached. A verb is not bound to be an expression either of the active voice or of the passive. And it can be the expression of an action without its being classified by grammarians as active in grammatical form. It can be, for example, deponent, that is to say grammatically passive but semantically active. In some languages, for instance Ancient Greek and Sanskrit, it can be grammatically middle-voiced where this means that while in the active voice a verb refers to a procedure or event outside the subject (e.g. Greek *louein*, to wash something), in the middle voice the verb refers to a procedure or event to which the subject is interior (e.g. Greek *louesthai*, to wash oneself), so the standard middle-voiced verb is not simply reflexive.[5] Even when a language seems to lack the formal category of the middle voice (also sometimes called medial diathesis), it can be rewarding to look for analogues that serve something like one or other of the purposes that the official middle voice serves, for instance to indicate that neither the speaker nor the addressee in a particular linguistic exchange is either the doer of a certain deed or the one to whom the deed is done. 'Suffering', a near-synonym for 'passion', can connote an active response to suffering, a bearing of it without complaining. In the terminology of Scotus and

Hopkins to suffer can be an act of will. Similarly 'reception' brings with it a nuance of responsive acceptance and a bi-directionality that is not captured in the paradigm of something's or someone's being physically as distinct from phenomenologically struck.

The bi-directionally cooperative pattern that complicates the physicalist model of passivity need not be the dialectical resultant of a coalescence of inward and outward impulses. It need not be a synthesis. To take another case, when I am attracted by something, to some degree I love it. Furthermore, although I am passive in relation to the thing's active attractive power, my loving it is conceptually inseparable from my actual or potential behaviour, typically my disposition to protect it from harm.

Respectful love is not a fusion. It is a chiasm, notwithstanding that one paradigm of what goes under that name is the reciprocal crossing of the optic nerves that is represented by a symmetrical upper case X. That paradigm case is binocular. It is the crossing of the paths of two nerves that have separate points of origin, one in each eye. But the upper-case letter X is also the capitalisation in Greek of the visibly asymmetrical lower-case χ. How to prevent this asymmetry being lost is a problem that remains to be resolved when from the optical paradigm we turn to the literary and rhetorical paradigm such as is exemplified by John F. Kennedy's injunction 'Ask not what your country can do for you – ask what you can do for your country?' The problem is: how to prevent chiasmus being turned into synthesis. It is posed too by the question of the relationship between intention and attention that will be taken up in our last chapter.

We are told in the Lexicon compiled by Hopkins' fellow Oxonians Henry Liddell and Robert Scott that the asymmetrical and slightly differently spelled *chiasma* represented by χ was used, as x or X are more commonly used in our time, to mark something that is spurious or wrong – for instance, that the total of a sum as calculated in a child's arithmetic exercise book is incorrect. Readers of Hopkins might consider this an appropriate sign to append to what he himself describes as the 'barbarous' neologisms created by him which will be encountered by readers of the following chapters. By way of encouragement once more, I remind those readers of the significance attributed implicitly by Goethe to the 'scare-' or 'shudder-'quotes (*Angst Zitate*) that such strange words earn when he has his Faust say (directing the actor to shudder as he says it) *Das Schaudern ist der Menschheit bestes Teil*, 'It is when they shudder that human beings are truest to themselves.'[6] By the time readers have reached the end of this book they will perhaps have learned that this human significance, as well as a more than human significance, extends to Scotus' metaphysics of formal distinction and to the 'aesthethics' (*sic*) based upon it by Hopkins the philosopher and philologist as his words are interpreted following the clues of chiasmus and the middle voice or something like it in the work on which we are about to embark.

What we are about to embark on is a *lecture expliquée* – what French scholars also call an *explication de texte*. It is a close reading and spelling out of certain sometimes outlandish words and of the syllables and letters of which they are composed read in their relationship to the sentences, paragraphs and wider contexts including titles and epigraphs. As another piece of jargon for this familiar phenomenon has it, this relationship exhibits a hermeneutic circularity. This circularity is one where the circles that display it are sometimes broken and sometimes spawn epicycles that overlap them or impinge on them or each other tangentially. This complication is flagged in the title of the final chapter. There, a trans- or quasi-transcendentality is announced in which a centrifugal transcendence is transcended by a centripetal one that, up to a certain point, overcomes it. This complexity is reflected in what Hopkins calls 'cleaves', playing on the Abelian character of this word with its penchant both towards 'split apart' and towards 'cling together'. It is detectable also in the criss-crossing between Scotus' tautly consecutive propositions with the hermeneutic zigzags that at once interrupt and favour the flow of his arguments. Centuries before Descartes takes time off to address his God midway through the course of the argument of the *Meditations* addressed to his *ego*, Scotus sews a prayer into the tightly woven fabric of his *ergos*. No less than Hopkins, Scotus is concerned to provoke in his reader a sense of 'as if for the first and last time'. That is one way of spelling out what they both mean by haecceity.

Making a cross reference of my own, I draw attention to the fact that a few sentences ago I stated that the complexity in the material that dictates this complexity in the format of our study of it is signalled in the title of the final chapter in which a certain trans- or quasi-transcendentality is announced. I could have said that this is 'annunciated' or 'Annunciated', borrowing an expression from the theology subscribed to by Scotus and Hopkins. Without endorsing it however. For midway through the exegesis of the conversation between these authors undertaken in this book allusions begin to be made to a notion of the religious that, I argue, does not necessarily derive its impetus from such institutional religions as that subscribed to by the authors mentioned in the book's title. These are allusions to the detailed presentations of this notion which I have made beyond this book's confines.[7] In the volume that is in process of getting underway I return to this notion only in order to demonstrate that the defence of it may be not only consistent with but also helped by what Scotus and Hopkins say regarding this study's crux: the proto-relation of thisness and formal distinction interpreted as a clue to the middle-voiced chiasmus of attention with intention.

These interconnected topics raise the question of the demand they and the two propounders of them just named make for an investigation of will. Chapter 12, from which we now begin to count down, pursues this question via an inquiry into what might be meant by the idea of willing not to will, *velle ut non velle*, interpreted in the light of the formula *amo: volo ut sis*, 'I love: I will that you be', taken as a guide to a construal of attention held in tension, in stress (and in what Hopkins will teach us to call instress) with intention.

Chapter 11 seeks to interpret the second of the Latin formulae just mentioned as an indication of an alternative to an appeal to a version of negative theology as means to achieving an exit from the absolute metaphysico-theological presuppositions which determine the questions asked by Scotus and Hopkins.

Chapter 10 resumes and develops the theme introduced in Chapter 2 of the verbality and adverbiality that willing introduces into the nominality of being.

Chapter 9 treats of the way existence as distinguished from essence is implicated in thisness.

Chapter 8 expounds Charles Sanders Peirce's attempt to give a partially Scotist account of the structures of modern science. His account continues to put more emphasis on practice than is allowed by Thomism and Aristotle. Its focus on the sciences makes it a foil for Hopkins' application of Scotism to the idioms of poetry.

Chapter 7 advertises the too little-known writings of John Alec Baker. These balance the accentuation of the poetic heard in Hopkins and the accentuation of the scientific imposed by Peirce. Without any explicit invocation of Scotus or Hopkins, Baker underlines the difference between the universalities at which the scientist aims and the more than particular singularities which the poet proclaims. While doing that he raises the question to what degree these apparent extremes cooperate, crossing the logical connective 'if-then' of scientific method with the logical connective 'as-if' of the poetic imagination. He also compels the reader to face the distinction between likeness or resemblance, the concept of which is especially alive in the sphere of the aspect of formal distinction that Scotus calls common nature, and, on the other hand, the conceit of individual identity marked by *haecceitas* and *ecceitas*. These are some of the reasons why Chapter 7 may be regarded as the crux at which the first part and the second part of the book intercept each other chiasmically.

Chapter 6 wonders whether the risk of adulteration run by Hopkins' embarrassingly frequent repetition of the word 'beauty' might have been averted by substituting for that word more frequently the word 'sublime', the word 'God' or the word 'Look', *ecce*.

The Crux

Chapter 5 comments on Heidegger's dissertation on Scotism.

Chapter 4 demonstrates how Scotus' conception of formal distinction supports Hopkins' distinction between inscape and instress.

Chapter 3 shows how the path for Hopkins' distinction between inscape and instress is prepared by his response to Parmenides' teaching on the togetherness of being and thinking.

Chapter 2 conducts a close reading of the *ipsissima verba* of texts in which Hopkins uses his neologisms 'inscape' and 'instress'.

Chapter 1, the brief introductory chapter now closing, is chiefly concerned to reaffirm that the crux of the study of Scotus and Hopkins which it introduces is the relation or proto-relation of the ipseity of thisness to formal distinction interpreted as a clue to the middle-voiced chiasmus of attention with intention. That is what cast the spell over Hopkins referred to in the title of this book. That is what casts its spell over this book's author. An *exploratio philosophica* of that and of the fascinating by-ways and highways of logic, metaphysics, ethics and aesthetics which it opens up, will occupy by far the majority of this volume's pages. But the final pages bring with them what some readers will regard as a bonus or grace or 'grace', and other readers as a disgrace. Whatever we call it (as Hopkins might say),[8] it takes the form of the discovery that, paradoxically, the philosophical exploration just referred to lends support to a notion of the religious or the 'religious' that is very different from the one adhered to by the two priests.

2
Instress Scaped and Inscape Stressed

'Inscape', and some of Hopkins' other neologisms, are set in contrast with one another in a paragraph in his journal dated 14 September 1871 where a remark made by Ruskin about a picture by Turner of the Pass of Faido leads him to ask 'What is the running instress, so independent of at least the immediate scape of the thing, which unmistakeably distinguishes and individuates things?'[1] I take the referent of the relative clause in this question to be the instress understood as the factor that makes individuation possible. He describes the instress as running because instress is not static. It is not static because it accompanies the history of a continuant through time. And it is not static because its own tension increases or decreases like the tension of the string of a musical instrument undergoing the process of being tuned. From Hopkins' early diaries it is obvious that he took delight in tracing or imagining etymologies, that is to say the histories of those entities we call words. He would have taken delight in pointing out that the word 'string' is connected etymologically with the Italian word *stringendo* which when written on a musical score means that a passage is to be played with accelerating tempo. This word may also be indirectly connected etymologically with the Latin root of 'contraction', a word that plays a crucial role, we shall see, in explaining why Hopkins fell under the spell of Duns Scotus.

The adjective 'running' may also be called for in order to describe the instress involved in the incident concerning Turner reported by Ruskin. A key feature of that incident is the retrospective foreshortening made possible by the fact that what is being described is a progression. Turner's and Hopkins' experience have in common the sudden realisation that they have earlier passed through a certain point on a journey. So the present stress becomes semi-detached from its immediate afternoon predecessor and semi-attached to the memory of the one already experienced – we could also say exerted – that morning. The painter and the poet are surprised to find themselves retraversing familiar surroundings.

The reference to the 'immediate scape' in Hopkins' question about the identity of the running instress is a reference to the qualities a thing can share with other things or a quality it may itself come to have or lose in the course of its history without its ceasing to be one and the same thing. The distinction between likeness and identity or re-identification matches the distinction between inscape or scape on the one hand and running instress on the other. This is what seems to be the message intended by the somewhat complex sentence with which the paragraph touching on Ruskin and Turner ends: 'I think it is this same running instress by which we identify or, better, test and refuse to identify with our various suggestions a thought which has just slipped from the mind at an interruption.' My interpretation of this sentence will be confirmed when in the next chapter I come to consider what Hopkins means by what he refers to as Parmenides' 'feeling for instress'.

But why in the clause 'so independent of at least the immediate scape of the thing' used by Hopkins to describe 'this running instress' is the noun 'scape' qualified by the adjective 'immediate'? And why in some places does he appear to write of scaping as if it were more superficial ('immediate') than inscape? In one place he uses the phrase 'husks and scapes', suggesting again a lack of depth.[2] In other contexts he seems to employ 'scape' as an abbreviation for 'inscape' used as a noun or as a verb. The word 'inscape' appears in the note on Parmenides written by Hopkins three years earlier than the journal entry of 1871 in which he poses the question we have just been discussing. This word's second syllable derives via Norman French from Late Latin *cappare*, from which derive also English 'cloak' and 'cape', words for garments that enable what they cover to escape our attention or to be only fleetingly perceived. Notwithstanding Hopkins' avowed or pretended ignorance of German, the contexts of his references to inscape suggest a possible Germanic etymology for 'scape' available to him at least via Anglo-Saxon through, for instance, 'landscape' and compounds he himself cites. Referring to his use of the word 'sakes' in the sonnet 'Henry Purcell' he tells Bridges in a letter dated 26 May 1879:

> *Sake* is a word I find it convenient to use: I did not know when I did so first that it is common in German, in the form *sach* [*sache*]. It is the sake of 'for the *sake* of', *forsake, namesake, keepsake*. I mean by it the being a thing has outside of itself, as a voice by its echo, a face by its reflection, a body by its shadow, a man by his name, fame, or memory, *and also* that in the thing by virtue of which especially it has this being abroad, and that is something distinctive, marked, specifically or individually speaking, as for a voice and echo clearness;

for a reflected image light, brightness; for a shadow-casting body bulk; for a man genius, great achievements, amiability, and so on. In this case it is, as the sonnet says, distinctive quality in genius.[3]

He writes 'being abroad', a gloss on the being a being has outside or beside itself, its identity dependent on something other than itself. He writes 'distinctive' and 'specifically or individually', thereby bequeathing to us the questions how the specifically distinctive is to be distinguished from the individually distinctive. Does Hopkins distinguish these two distinctions? Does not his phrase 'distinctive *quality*' suggest that what he says about inscape and instress is at cross purposes with what Scotus says about formal distinction and haecceity? These questions will be taken up when it has been learned in Chapter 4 what Scotus means by *distinctio formalis*.

Later chapters will follow up the notions of likeness, image and representation implied in the illustrations listed in this letter from Hopkins to Bridges. In particular, adding the notions of metaphor and analogy to this list, an attempt will be made to shed light on the relation between scientific or otherwise factual truth and the grammar of poetry or the otherwise literary and artistic.

Hopkins championed Anglo-Saxon. So too did the poet William Barnes. It is sometimes said that it was from Barnes that Hopkins obtained the idea of what he called 'sprung rhythm'. This is improbable given the publication dates of works by Barnes and of what Hopkins regarded as examples of sprung rhythm in his own works.[4] However, Hopkins knew Barnes' studies of Anglo-Saxon.[5] In one of them he could have consulted a glossary containing many expressions of the kind he, Hopkins himself, used, for example: 'upgather', 'foretake', 'upcleave', 'cohere', 'oncleave', 'adhere', 'hearsomeness', 'obedience', 'faith-hear', 'enthusiasm', 'withstalling', 'antithesis'.[6] Although a word for 'landscape' does not appear in Barnes' list, there can be little doubt that that word's second syllable, along with 'scope', brings with it the sense of making or effecting or creating. 'Scape' or 'scap' is cognate with German *schaffen*, *Schaft*, *Schöpfung* (creation or Creation, the condition of being or having been made) and with English 'shape'.

This last word invites invocation of the family of terms derived from Latin *forma* which is central to the theological and metaphysical doctrines to which Hopkins would have been introduced through his study of Aquinas and, reaching back to Greek *eidos*, of Plato and Aristotle. It will therefore play a pivotal part in our understanding of how Hopkins' ontology both inherits and diverges from that of these other thinkers. So too will the word 'creation'. 'I have been thinking about creation', he writes at the beginning of his Comments on *The Spiritual Exercises* of St Ignatius

Loyola (circa 1881),[7] one of his most revealing pieces of philosophical prose. Among the reasons why that piece is so revealing is that the notion of creation contemplated in it spans the apparent gap between a verb standing for a causal action and a noun standing for a thing or a fact or a state of affairs brought into existence or a resulting effect or event or performance. That that apparent gap is only apparent is one of the lessons we shall learn from the Comments. We have begun to learn this lesson as soon as we realise that the words 'existence' and *ek-sisto* already contain the sense of 'brought about' or 'caused'.[8] Thus they bring with them a metaphysical or metaphysico-theological assumption, even if the implied cause or ground is the cause or ground of itself, so one with and other than itself.

In the *Metaphysics*, the work Hopkins will admit he regretfully returned to its place on the library shelf, Aristotle draws a distinction between form and matter. But it is not on account of this distinction favoured by Aristotle and Aquinas that Hopkins turns away from them towards Scotus. Neither Scotus nor Hopkins rejects the distinction Aristotle makes in Book Zeta of his *Metaphysics* between predicative form or essence and prime matter understood as that of which form is predicated but which is itself not predicable of anything. The complaint made by Scotus and Hopkins is that although in terms of this distinction an account can be given of the resemblance between one thing and another, it gives no account or recognition of the identity a thing cannot share with another and of the cause or ground of such identity whose thisness Scotus calls *haecceitas*.

Is 'inscape' Hopkins' equivalent for Scotus' *haecceitas*? No, as will be shown below. Nevertheless, an affirmative answer to this question might appear to be correct if 'inscape' and 'scape' are taken as synonymous respectively with 'instress' and 'stress' as these expressions are employed in Hopkins' Comments under Loyola's heading *Principium sive Fundamentum*. The word 'inscape' occurs in these comments but with nothing like the frequency of occurrence of the words 'instress' and 'stress'. The latter pair raises the question, analogous to the one touched on earlier with regard to the pair 'inscape' and 'scape', whether the form with the prefix always stands for something deep, as Hopkins states explicitly that it does sometimes. Does the pair 'instress' and 'stress' mark a difference of meaning as well as of spelling? One matter that is beyond doubt here is that there are degrees of stress and instress. This is evident from his employment of these notions in the Comments to explicate the experience of selfhood and selving in the case of the human and especially one's own self. But are degrees of stress or instress or pitch degrees of depth? Depth of what? Of personality? We shall wait to see what Hopkins will have to say about that.

He remarks in his journal that in the presence of another person (he mentions a day on which he was out walking accompanied by his colleague Herbert Lucas) 'instress cannot come'.[9] This does not mean that instress cannot pertain to the will. For, like Scotus, Hopkins distinguishes passive natural will from active rational will. As these last words suggest, and as we shall explain further in Chapter 4 and elsewhere, active will and intellect are 'formally distinct but really inseparable'. This mantra is a key to understanding how both Scotus and Hopkins can agree with Aquinas that will and intellect are psychologically equiprimordial yet, as in this respect followers of Augustine, disagree with Aquinas' teaching that intellect is metaphysically and theologically prior.

In another journal entry Hopkins writes: 'standing before the gateway I had an instress . . .'[10] This could lead one to think that having an instress is something like experiencing a hot flush or a throb of toothache. The experience could equally well be described more grandly as an epiphany. That Hopkins would describe it as an apocalypse and a grace is suggested by the apposition he makes in his sentence 'The first intention then of God outside himself, as they say, *ad extra*, outwards, the first outstress of God's power, was Christ.' It seems correct to take 'intention' here in the sense that implies will and ultimately love, another topic of which we shall have more to say in due course. Outstress is a person's or a Person's expression of instress, an instance of the doing that expresses his or her being, according to the ergontology that we shall discover Hopkins reads in or into the poem of Parmenides. Further, rather as, in the realm of the personal, 'outstress' and its cognates are substituted for the over-familiar terms 'will' and 'intention' that belong to the traditional terminology of philosophy and theology, so too in the discourse of personal behaviour and non-personal 'behaviour' the threadbare words 'appearance', 'representation' and 'presence' ask to be replaced by the newly forged word 'outscape' used in Hopkins' journal entry recording that 'In the afternoon we took the train for Paris and passed through a country of pale grey rocky hills of a strong and simple outscape covered with fields of wormy green vines.'[11] Notwithstanding these rewordings of the world and of man's workings within it, outstress and instress and stress can vary in strength and pitch. Hence in certain circumstances they may, like Leibniz's subliminal *petites perceptions*, sink below the degree needed for them to be noticeably felt. Similarly, outscape and inscape may be so deep that they escape our attention, though the articulation of the very complex relation of attention to intention will eventually reveal itself to have been among the final tasks taken up in this book.

Hopkins describes in his journal an experiment in which a duck is held for a while on a table upon the surface of which, out from the bird's beak or transversely, chalk marks are inscribed. As long as the bird keeps its eyes on these marks she does not attempt to raise her head. When the bird is then placed on another table, one without such marks, she still does not attempt to raise her head. This, according to one hypothesis, is because the bird, 'keeping the abiding offscape of the hand grasping her neck fancies she is still held down'. The expression 'abiding offscape' is Hopkinsese for what in oldstyle is called memory. So it denotes an example of the chiasmic structural (and 'structuralist') interdependence of identity and unidentity mentioned in the passage cited earlier in which Hopkins expounds the forces of 'sake'.

Hopkins remains unconvinced by this first explanation. A more plausible one, he suggests, is 'the fascinating instress of the straight white line'.[12] We might have expected him to say that what the bird finds fascinating is an inscape. For we are testing how far we can press the reading of Hopkins that regards the family of scape words as fresh substitutes for the time-honoured technical terminology of representation, appearances, views, presentation, etc., and regards the family of stress words as 'flush' transcriptions of the jargon of free will, choice, intention and so on. Also time-honoured, however, is the intrication of the familiar predecessors of the scape and stress families of coinages. How, otherwise, could there have been all those arguments in the history of philosophy for and against the primacy of understanding and the primacy of the will, not to mention the dismantling of these arguments that is effected by introducing into them the notion of equiprimordiality? We shall find cause to remember – to keep an 'abiding offscape' of – Hopkins' gradualist conceptions of freedom and perfection of will and of what, in the wake of Scotus' *gradus*, he names 'pitch'. These are conceptions that seem not to restrict will and personality or soul to the spheres of the divine and the human (and the angelic), anymore than does Aristotle with his hierarchy of rational, sensitive and vegetative varieties or aspects of the psyche.

When I say that Hopkins does not seem to impose the restriction just mentioned, I mean only that he is as ready to speak in shudder-quotes or analogically of 'personality' and 'soul' outside the spheres of the paradigmatically human and divine (and angelic) as he is to speak of the 'behaviour' of beings outside these spheres. This analogical application of these quidditive class terms is compatible with his endorsement of Scotus' teaching, against the doctrine of the analogy of being taught by Henry of Ghent and Aquinas, that the transcendental term 'being' holds univocally of the ways of being of creatures and the Creator.[13]

Subito probas eum, Hopkins writes, echoing 'What is man . . . that thou shouldst visit him every morning, and suddenly put him to the test?, before he is fully awake' (Job 7: 17–18).[14] If that is how the Creator announces himself to us, we might expect that when his creatures announce themselves they too do so all of a sudden. This is the way Hopkins describes how the inscapes of the world come to our notice. They are not 'perceived' (from *percepi*). Rather do they take or catch our eye, catch (from *capere*) our attention. Sometimes they are less perceived than sensed in that they intimate something difficult of access and because the inscape will be sensed in its profundity only if there is an increase in the *energeia* of stress. 'Unless you refresh the mind from time to time you cannot always remember or believe how deep in things the inscape is.'[15] Hence 'The bluebells in your hand baffle you with their inscape, made to every sense.'[16] It is as if, when he speaks of how deep in things the inscape is, the deepening is like the compression of a geometrical line to a point, or the conversion of a common noun into a proper name. Such a conversion carried to its extreme would close down the possibility of communication if by communication is meant the conveyance of a message from one person to another in the way you might pass the salt to a fellow diner. If communication is understood in that way the increase of depth and density would be simultaneously a decrease of information transmitted, a decrease to a zero point such as is envisaged in the statement: 'One feels that if it were possible to write poems without language, she would be content. What she is after is the unmediated – nothing, including words, must get in the way of what she sees.'[17] Step beyond that brink and the most you'll be able to do is repeat Antisthenes' tautological 'This is this.'[18] But for Hopkins the words 'poems without language' are a contradiction in terms. For him words are among the things the poet sees or hears, components of what the poet has made with sounds or marks. The composition joins two distinct factors: indexicality and common nature. In such naked indexicals as 'this' every vestige of common nature is threatened with obliteration. But not every mark or sound. For how without these could the poem aspire to the destiny Hopkins envisages for it of becoming music or dance? Becoming. Hopkins holds that every created thing, including his own 'selving', is in process of *fieri*, becoming, therefore partial. For him creation is continuous. It is at the same time discontinuous, in the way that the speech of the child or the foreigner who is learning a language, and of the aged native speaker who is losing hold of it, may lapse away from conventional patterns. Such wandering[19] can, however, be deliberate, as it frequently is in the writings of Hopkins when one grammatical practice is brought into conflict with another, and as it may be too when in the middle of a sequence of sentences about a certain nowness described by Dennis Potter in one of his last interviews he departs from the expected sequence of tenses.[20] I reproduce his words verbatim in order to preserve the pathos of the ungrammaticality of the sentences and unsentences from which his meaning rises like the plum tree of which he talks rises from the uncultivated soil. Or, in the sculpture by Rodin known as 'La Création de l'homme', like the clay taking shape from the hand that holds it up and like the hand itself reaching up from the clay.

> When I'm working in Ross, for example, there at this season, the blossom is out in full now, there in the west early. It's a plum tree, it looks like apple blossom but it's white, and looking at it, instead of saying 'Oh that's nice blossom' . . . last week looking at it through the window when I'm writing, I see it is the whitest, frothiest, blossomest blossom that there ever could be, and I can see it. Things are both more trivial than they ever were, and more important than they ever were, and the difference between the trivial and the important doesn't seem to matter. But the nowness of everything is absolutely wondrous, and if people could see that, you know. There's no way of telling you; you have to experience it, but the glory of it, if you like, the comfort of it, the reassurance . . . not that I'm interested in reassuring people – bugger that. The fact is, if you see the present tense, boy do you see it! And boy can you celebrate it.

He is looking at the tree and the tree seems to be looking back at him. A chiasmic crossover comes to pass. And 'blossomest' marks a crossing of a noun and an adjective. So perhaps it does not open up as deep a chasm as is opened up by Potter's 'full now' understood as an adjective followed by a noun rather than as a doubly adverbial 'fully now'. It definitely does not bring about as violent a chiasmic catastrophe as, referring in 'The Windhover' to the flight of the kestrel, is exemplified by Hopkins' phrase 'the achieve of'. In this phrase what is usually a verb borrows the force of a noun, and vice versa. In this phrase, we might say, adapting another word from that poem, grammar is buckled. Hopkins' word is 'Buckle!' with an exclamation mark. It could be an imperative, like the imperative 'Look' of the advice Wittgenstein gives in the *Philosophical Investigations*, 'don't think, but look',[21] or like Hopkins'

> Look, look: a May-mess, like on orchard boughs![22]

Potter says of his superlatively sublime blossomest blossom 'There's no way of telling you; you have to experience it', so that the three occasions where he mentions looking are implicitly imperatival and exclamatory. They say *ecce*! And they say it with regard to a non-human being.

Hopkins is speaking, however, of a human being, his own being, when he writes: 'Nothing else in nature comes near this unspeakable stress of pitch, distinctiveness, and selving . . .'[23] But we have observed that he uses the terms 'stress', 'instress' and 'pitch' at least analogically of non-human beings. A readiness to do this must be assumed if his references to instress and stress are to be seen as part of a defence of a notion of singularity that would not be vulnerable to the criticism levelled by Hegel in the *Phenomenology of Mind* against the doctrines of sensible certainty and self-certainty. These are the doctrines according to which the fullest reality belongs to, respectively, immediate sensory experience and immediate experience of self. Hegel's arguments against these doctrines consist in showing that ultimate reality cannot be the immediacy allegedly expressed in terms of, respectively, 'this' or 'I' or 'now'. These words are token reflexives, indexicals, shifters. Hence, as the last of them says most explicitly, they may pick out different things when used at different times or places. Therefore, Hegel goes on to demonstrate, the alleged ontological primacy of immediacy turns out to be mediated by categories of understanding and reason culminating in absolute being.

Hegel is addressed by Heidegger in *Being and Time*. An earlier work by Heidegger addresses Duns Scotus. What is said in these works is therefore relevant to the question whether the selves of which Hopkins writes range over not only human and superhuman entities but also over entities of the purely natural world and artefacts made by humans. We have already begun to find reason to say that they embrace all beings, not least because they take up the question of being as such. Heidegger's concentration on the question of being ministers to and is ministered to by a certain concern with beings. This is a concern that is witnessed to, for instance, both in his later poietic thinking (*dichtendes Denken*) and in a footnote in the Postscript to *What is Metaphysics?*[24] Likewise with Hopkins. Although his ordination into the priesthood marks a point at which his writings shift from being predominantly concerned with the natural world to being predominantly directed towards the life of the spirit,[25] these poles are mediated for him by the Incarnation. In the first paragraph of the Comments there takes place a redirecting of attention from 'the world without' ('the consideration commonly dwelt on' by philosophers, theologians and laymen) to 'the world within' considered by Augustine, Ignatius and Descartes. But the exterior continues to be considered from the perspective of the interior. Hopkins continues to be concerned with the gamut of beings of all pitches on the Great Scale of Being. The temperature of his concern with the metaphysics of Being is raised by his discovery of Scotus. Before turning to that *doctor subtilis*, we turn to the pages in which Hopkins reflects on how the metaphysical interest in Being is manifested by Parmenides, and how Parmenides puts Hopkins in a state of readiness to receive signals from Scotus. The phrase 'metaphysical interest in Being' is pleonastic in so far as 'metaphysics' is defined by Scotus as the science of Being and the other transcendentals to be investigated below in Chapter 5 and Chapter 6.[26]

3

Parsing the Poem of Parmenides

If we use the word 'Being' to translate Parmenides' *tò eón* as that English word was used at the time when while an undergraduate at Oxford Hopkins wrote his piece on that thinker's poem, we should heed John Burnet's observation that 'Parmenides does not say a word about "Being" anywhere... We must not render *tò eón* by "Being", *das Sein* or *l'être*. It is "What is", *das Seiende, ce qui est*. As (*tò*) *eînai* it does not occur, and hardly could occur at this date.'[1] We have seen that in that article on Parmenides Hopkins speaks both of instress or stress and of inscape. Facing his readers with the task of refining their conception of the relation of inscape to instress – but also now with the further task of deciphering two other unplain new words – he writes of Parmenides: 'His feeling for instress, for the flush and foredrawn and for inscape is most striking...'[2] Bearing on the question of the relation to each other of 'instress' and 'inscape' unravelled in our second chapter, and keeping in mind what was said in the first about the two-facedness of 'unravelling', it should be noted that the second 'and' in the sentence just cited and the fact that the sentence does not have 'or' could be held to imply that 'instress' and 'inscape' are not to be taken as synonyms. Yet, depending on whether the force of 'or' is exclusive (Latin *vel*) or non-exclusive (Latin *aut*), synonymity of the words 'instress' and 'inscape' is not necessarily implied either by the 'or' in Hopkins' statement a few lines later that: 'I have often felt... and felt the depth of an instress or how fast the inscape holds a thing that nothing is so pregnant and straightforward to the truth as simple *yes* and *is*.' This 'yes' and this 'is' refer back to 'things are' (or 'there are') and 'there is truth', phrases he has just offered along with 'it is' and 'there are' as transliterations of Parmendes' *éstin* and *tò eón*. So although other functions may appear to be performed by the term 'instress' (and 'stress') in other places, for instance in the poem 'The Wreck of the Deutschland', in the paper on Parmenides this term serves to fill out Hopkins' reading of the Greek thinker's theory of the tie between thinking and being. The term 'tie' means what is meant by the Old French and the Latin terms from which arise the English word 'stress'. It stands for the binding and coupling of, for example, a name with a predicate, and for the identity of the bearer of the name or of the item indicated by the deictic pronouns 'This' and 'That'. You could never think or say what was not, because

> there would be no bridge, no stem of stress between us and things to bear us out and carry the mind over: without stress we might not and could not say Blood is red but only This blood is red or The last blood I saw was red nor even that, for in later language not only universals would not be true but the copula would break down even in particular judgments.[3]

This passage attempts to convey what Hopkins means by 'unforedrawn', hence by 'foredrawn', in the second of the two above-mentioned new challenges he presents to his readers' hermeneutic perspicacity. The key is his statement that 'Not-being is here seen as want of oneness, all that is unforedrawn, waste space which offers nothing to the eye to foredraw or many things foredrawing away from one another': the many uncoincident with and unsubsumed or uncontracted by a principle of unity, unthought through a really existing universal and, to echo a translation favoured by J. Hillis Miller,[4] not chiming together or rhyming ('All beauty may by a metaphor be called rhyme')[5] or, as Parmenides himself says, without *sunechesthai*, without being bound or drawn together, gathered or synthesised.[6]

To foredraw is to think or perceive, *noein*.[7] This is to grasp not only universals or essences (*essentia*) in their anticipative, predelineative or 'foredrawing' capacity. It is also to posit entities (*entia*) in the undistributable singularity of their momentary or continuant real existence. As Hopkins is encouraged to say by Parmenides and, we shall see, by Scotus, without the entitivity of *entia*, and with a nounhood isolated from a verbhood centred on the verb 'to be', thinking would fall short of metaphysical and natural *scientia*, because thinking would fall short of sameness in difference – thinking would fall short of itself.[8]

To say this and to say what is said in the passage just reproduced from the *Note-Books* is, ironically, to say very much what Hegel says about sense-certainty and self-certainty, except that to the Parmenidean thesis that to think and to be are the same Hegel adds that sheer being and sheer non-being are the same too because they are both absolutely indeterminate. There is further irony in the kinship with Aristotle and Aquinas manifested by the sentences cited, for we shall be told by Hopkins that it was 'with sorrow' that he returned the former's *Metaphysics* to the library shelf at Stonyhurst, and neither he nor his new hero Scotus was seeking to undermine the Aristotelian and Thomist accounts wholesale. They both wanted to supplement those accounts of the possibility of generic and specific being with an account that allowed the possibility of individualised being through a certain 'contraction'.

Parmenides' thesis that 'it is the same thing that can be thought and that can be' may well hold of absolutely determinate entities, however we interpret such determinacy. But Parmenides himself makes no special mention of such entities. Nor does Hopkins in his pages on the poem of Parmenides. The particularity of the particular judgements he does mention there is that of instances of determinable universals. It is not what he understands by uniquely determinate individuality or what Scotus understands by *haecceitas*, eachness or thisness.

This topic of thisness is raised only by implication in the pages of Hopkins' essay on Parmenides on which we have commented so far. Hence neither there nor in our own pages so far has much progress been made towards providing an answer to the question whether Hopkins' word 'inscape' is, as is sometimes said or assumed, synonymous with Scotus' word *haecceitas*. Some small progress in that direction has been made, however, for we have begun to recognise that, at least in the context of his comments on Parmenides' affirmation of the sameness of what is and what is thought, Hopkins' references to inscape are distinguished from his references to instress in that the latter play a more fundamental part than the former in his account of the Parmenidean affirmation of sameness. That this is so is already intimated in his second paragraph when of what he calls Parmenides' great text he writes that it means, 'perhaps one can say, a little over-defining his meaning . . . that all things are upheld by instress and are meaningless without it'. On the evidence of the Comments on Ignatius and the commentary on Parmenides, stress and instress figure predominently when Hopkins is considering issues of theological and philosophical ontology. At one stage in his account he even places a reference to stress in apposition to a reference to Being:

> The truth in thought is Being, stress, and each word is one way of acknowledging Being and each sentence by its copula *is* (or its equivalent) the utterance and assertion of it.[9]

It sometimes looks as though stress and instress uphold or support the scape or inscape of things, where upholding says in an Anglo-Saxon way what Latin says as *substans* or *suppositio* and what Greek says as *hypokeimenon* or *hypostates*. In the Aristotelian and Scholastic traditions these classical terms are widely used of prime matter defined as that of which what makes up the forms of things is predicated without itself being predicable of anything. This thought raises the question whether we would be 'overdefining his meaning' if we agreed that Hopkins' word 'inscape' is an Anglo-Saxonism for the classical terms *forma* and *eidos*. This possibility compels us to fill a gap left in a sentence we cited earlier in order to express an opinion there on the force of the word 'and' that occurs in it. Made whole, the sentence in question says that Parmenides' 'feeling for instress, for the flush and foredrawn [referred to also three pages later as 'the mind's grasp – *noein*, the foredrawing act'] and for inscape is most striking and from this one can understand Plato's reverence for him as the great father of Realism': Papa Parmenides. Here, by implication, Realism must be understood as the doctrine that universals are not subjective inventions of the human mind, and that at least some of them, those of which Plato says they are Forms or Ideas, exist objectively and 'transcendentally' in their own right though not independently of mentality.[10]

'Reverence' in the paragraph just cited has overtones of the paganly or otherwisely religious. This is consistent with Hopkins' remark at the beginning of the paragraph that it is 'with religious conviction' that Parmenides repeats his great text. Noteworthy too in this connection is his use of the word 'faith' to translate *pistis* in Parmenides' phrase *pistis alēthēs*, 'unerring (true) faith', and in Parmenides' sentence 'Nor yet is there any force of faith will grant that from Being (the one) can ever come anything side by side with it', the many or the not-being that is represented by the as yet unshaped, unscaped clay from which emerges the hand in Rodin's sculpture representing the creation of man, whether in a 'subjective' or 'objective' sense of this 'of'. The religious tone sounds when Hopkins attributes 'an undetermined Pantheist idealism' to Parmenides, for whose word ἐόν the best translation is sometimes 'god'. Perhaps Hopkins' consciousness that his own Christian faith resonates in his commentary on Parmenides is what leads him to remark that he may be 'a little overdefining' Parmenides' meaning.

That we are not over-defining Hopkins' meaning in our reading of him so far is confirmed by his remark that 'in the world, besides natures or essences or "inscapes" and the selves, supposits, hypostases, or, in the case of rational natures, persons which wear and 'fetch' or instance them, there is still something else – fact or fate'.[11] We have found reason to connect selves directly with stress and instress as these are given prominence in the comments on Ignatius and explicative of the 'to be' and of the act of affirmation given prominence in the comment on Parmenides. Over against selves, hence over against those selves that are persons, inscape has more to do with what is affirmed and what something is affirmed about. 'Inscape' embraces the manifold of things Hopkins considers it his duty to praise in his songs of the created natural world; 'what I am in the habit of calling inscape is what I above all aim at in poetry', he writes to Bridges on 15 February 1879 in a letter in which his neologism is put in apposition to design in painting, to melody in music, to pattern in both and, of course, to pattern in the poem and in whatever in the world is the poem's *motif*, that is to say, as Cézanne would say, in what moves the painter to pick up his brush and the poet to pick up his pen. Hopkins adds: 'Now it is the virtue of design, pattern, or inscape to be distinctive and it is the vice of distinctiveness to become queer.' Anticipating a time when his poetry will, he hopes, have taken on 'a more balanced and Miltonic style', he is prepared meanwhile still to risk erring on the side of oddness in order to overcome the thing's reluctance to show itself that is implied already in calling something an inscape. For although the inscaped is the distinctive, the distinctive is not the obvious. It may require the sometimes forceful application of the technical skills of the painter, the composer or the poet to bring its distinctiveness out. This holds not only for, say, the things of the natural world of which the poet's words speak, but also for the words themselves. They too have inscapes, for instance the very word 'inscape', a word we should therefore be prepared to have such difficulty understanding as we are indeed having here.

So inscape may speak unto inscape. Inscapes may rhyme. One inscape may, to borrow a word from Scotus, 'communicate' with another inscape. However, an inscape may only ever be *glimpsed*. It happens suddenly, *exaiphnēs*. Its manner of being seen is to be *noticed* or *caught* or suddenly caught *by*: 'my eye was suddenly caught by the scaping of the leaves that grow in alleys and avenues: I noticed it first in an elm and then in limes.'[12] He says this in the context of that reference to the inscapes of the world he aims to find words for in his poetry. But as well as inscape 'worded', there is inscape of the acoustic or graphic consonants, vowels and syllables of which the words are made up. Inscape is sounded, drawn or painted. Was capturing the inscape in a drawing or painting perhaps what Turner was hoping but first failing to do when, as reported by his fellow traveller in Italy Robert James Graves, he made a sketch of a cloudscape, discarded it, tried again, discarded it, until at the third attempt he exclaimed 'There it is'? Maybe these words hit upon the inscape of what is said by Parmenides' word for what there is.

The adolescent Hopkins entertained the hope of becoming a painter. Hence when he speaks of 'catching' or just failing to capture an inscape, he sometimes means 'capturing' and reproducing it in the sketches he himself draws to illustrate or augment his verbal descriptions. These drawings may be no less 'foredrawings' than the thoughts conveyed by those verbal descriptions. And they may be withdrawings of a family likeness which the artist is trying to bring out but which is playing hard to get. Speaking of a brook, he writes in the late summer or early autumn of 1872, 'I caught an inscape as flowing and well marked almost as the frosting on glass and slabs; but I could not reproduce it afterwards with the pencil.' The notion of flowing or running, here of an inscape of water rather than a running instress, is one Hopkins applies to inscapes as such, for instance when – incidentally demonstrating that his admiration of Parmenides is compatible with an admiration of Heraclitus (his admiration for Pythagoras is witnessed to in his musical ideal of poetry) – Hopkins writes a year earlier: 'A beautiful instance of inscape sided on the slide, that is successive sidings of one inscape, is seen in the behaviour of the flag flower from the shut bud to the full blowing: each term you can distinguish is beautiful in itself and of course if the whole "behaviour" were gathered up in itself and so stalled it would have a beauty of all the higher degree.' The extreme of such gathering up would be, to use the term Scotus uses, the 'contraction' of such serial qualitative sidings to sheer thisness beyond *qua*-ness. The gathering up Hopkins envisages here, however, does not stretch that far. It does not make this metaphysical leap beyond the representation of the growth of a living creature as this is effected by time-lapse photography.

That photographic technique had not yet been discovered, but Muybridge began his experiments with freeze frames of a running horse (compare Avicenna's *horseness*)[13] in the very year, 1872, in which Hopkins records his failed experiment to represent in a pencilled drawing the inscape of the flowing brook. Whether he had more success with other attempts to capture inscape in a drawing can be decided only by looking at his drawings or at reproductions of them in the journals and notebooks, and only if we can satisfy ourselves that we have glimpsed what he means by an inscape. In the interim, of his success at least in representing the overlapping of temporal phases there is ample proof in the metrical and musical patterns of so much of his verse with its torrents of commas, colons and semi-colons but ne'er an internal full stop to allow his reader a chance to draw breath. It is as though he wants to make sure that we are out of breath while we are reading out his poems, an effect like that which Emily Dickinson creates with all those dashes ('think-strokes') that her early editors refused to take seriously, or like that created by the often almost stifled utterance of the word 'beautiful',[14] as though it were a word looking for a meaning.

Further evidence of how seriously Hopkins takes sonic repetition is his experiments with what he calls sprung rhythm. One of the features of this device is a predominance of adjacent accented sounds that confer a stronger than usual sense of forward drive. It is akin to one of the kinds of alliterative *cynghanedd* (harmonious chime) practised in the Welsh poetry at which Hopkins himself tried his hand. Here, not his most successful poem, is an English approximation to that kind:

> Repeat that, repeat,
> Cuckoo, bird, and open ear wells, heart-springs, delightfully sweet,
> With a ballad, with a ballad, a rebound
> Off trundled timber and scoops of the hillside ground, hollow
> hollow hollow ground:
> The whole landscape flushes on a sudden at a sound.

The whole inscape of the landscape, if an inscape could ever be whole, is what we might be tempted to call its essence, but that term is for Hopkins too liable to conjure up a traditionally philosophical conceptuality that freezes the flux, robs the 'on a sudden' flush and flash of its freshness and reduces the 'movie' shot to a photographic 'still'. Recall Heidegger's 'As for me, I never really stare at the landscape','*Ich selbst betrachte eigentlich die Landschaft gar nie.*'[15] To do that is to stunt the growth and to neglect the flush implied in *phusein*, the Ancient Greek word for what philosophers as early as Averrhoes distinguish as living, acting and present participial *natura naturans* in contrast with nominally, statically and past participial *natura naturata*. To focus attention on the view is to do something like what Wittgenstein, in a remark we shall cite in the next chapter, likened to detaching the skin from an object, turning it into what some philosophers would call a sense-datum, as though it were a second object subsisting in its own right.

The Scholastic term 'essence' would stop in its tracks what in the earlier quotation is called 'behaviour'. Hopkins places this latter term within shudder-quotes because it is used here of natural selves that, like those expressed in the 'lovely behaviour of silk-sack clouds' in the sonnet 'Hurrahing in Harvest', have a lower pitch than the selves he describes at least once as rational natures or persons, where a person is defined as 'a rational (that is intellectual) supposit, the supposit of a rational nature'.[16]

The English term 'nature' can be understood generally as approximately synonymous with the term 'essence', where either of these terms is taken as the name of something material or non-material or as a combination of both. Understood more specifically it connotes the natural world as contrasted with the non-natural, where the non-natural is the divine or the human or the cultural or the personal (or the angelic). To the personal, Hopkins ascribes a priority over the natural due to its being endowed with a capacity to exercise free will such that where non-personal things 'behave', persons *do*.[17] Doing is their way of being, of way-making and making way. (As Heidegger would say, it is their *Seinsweise*, their *Be-wegung* and their being *unterwegs*.) Hopkins endeavours to show this

25

by proposing the barbarism 'doing be' derived from the familiar syntax according to which we move from a simple statement like 'he said' to the emphatic – *stressed* – form of the auxiliary verb in 'he did say' or of the corresponding Welsh *Efe a ddywedodd* that Hopkins also gives. 'Doing be' is a verbal noun. Compare the German verbal noun *Sein*, 'Be-*ing*', which, without abandoning the subject of ontology treated in Hopkins' comment on Parmenides, emphasises the inseparability of the 'to be', the 'it is' and the 'there is' from the will implicit in the affirmation of the radical Yes that these utterances express.

For Parmenides 'to be', 'it is' and 'there is' are affirmations of what purports to be the case: a matter of fact. This is a thesis that is underlined in the discussion of what in his classic study *The Route of Parmenides* Alexander Mourelatos calls 'the veridical "Is"'.[18] This thesis is endorsed by Hopkins, though it is partially obscured by the above-mentioned employment of the term 'Being' for τὸ ἐόν in the translation he used. This endorsement needs to be remembered if we are to grasp what is meant by the third member in the tripartition cited above of which we have so far commented only on the first two members, to wit stress or instress and inscape.

Beyond stress or instress and inscape, Hopkins says, 'there is still something else – fact or fate'. Fate is included among the woes and wells catalogued in the pivotal 'I find myself . . .' paragraphs of the Comments on Ignatius. 'All my fate', he says, eschatologically. In light of his fascination by questions of etymology, it is likely that he hoped his reader would hear in the word 'fact' a resonance of the past participle of *facere*, to do or to make, and in the word 'fate' a resonance of *fari*, to say. Saying too is a way of doing or making. It is the performance of an act of speech. When he links 'fact' and 'fate' together three times in one paragraph, once by 'or', once by 'and', and once by means of apposition, he is not treating these words either carelessly or carefully as equivalents. He is not unaware that 'fact' derives from the Latin past participle *factus* and that although 'fate' conveys the idea of a time in the past when something was dictated or inscribed ('the writing on the wall'), it also refers to the future. Something is fore-ordained. Something is predestined. That is to say, the 'something else' announced as a third member of his triad by Hopkins after his introduction of the notions of inscape and instress is the twofold notion of a future-oriented past, something predestined or Predestined.

At the point in his Comments on Loyola's *Spiritual Exercises* where his consideration of inscape and instress becomes a discussion of the third member of the trio, namely the disjunction fact-or-fate, the reader is jolted into recognising that the *Principium sive Fundamentum* referred to in the first heading of the Comments is not only a theoretical principle of ontology and epistemology and intellect. It is also a practical principle of moral and general theology. It is a principle that has to do with doing, a principle that, at least where rational mortals are concerned, has to do with the will. This does not mean that it has nothing to do with being. That would hardly be credible given Hopkins' admiration for Parmenides. Already in his comments on Parmenides he declines to accept the traditional opposition between being and doing. That is the force of the expression 'doing be' whose barbarous character he admits. This force is not as apparent in his comments on Parmenides as it is in the Comments on Ignatius. But it is there in the former. The aspect of doing in being is detectable in unamplified allusions to 'the foredrawing act' and 'The way men judge'.[19] 'Drawing' is cognate with Scotus' term 'contraction'. Judging implicates the will and all that Scotus will be found to have said and that Hopkins will go on to say about the role the will and instress play in thinking or knowing or perception (*noein, νοειν*). Then too there is choice in the realms of prudence, ethics, aesthetics, religion, life and love wherever justice and injustice of judgement are at stake, as they will be in later chapters of this study.

The point of the hyphenation in being-doing is spoken and spelled out less barbarously in the following lines from Hopkins' poem 'As kingfishers catch fire':

Each mortal thing does one thing and the same:
Deals out that being indoors each one dwells;
Selves – goes itself, *myself* it speaks and spells;
Crying *What I do is me: for that I came.*

Not *cogito ergo sum*, but *agere ergo sum*, or *volo ergo sum*, 'I will therefore I am.' At least where the I myself is the mortal human self, the person as distinguished from the beings in the great chain of being for whom doing seems to Hopkins to belong to a lower 'grade' or 'pitch' of 'behaviour' along with the kingfishers that catch fire and the dragonflies that draw flame, not to mention the stones that ring referred to earlier in the poem, those entities not included in the Aristotelian and Thomist scale of forms or formalities of souls: rationality, sensitivity and vegetivity. As for stones, we shall find ourselves drawn to another poet, indeed another 'Thomist', who shares a concern for them with Hopkins, and with Hopkins a desire to stress the first word of the verse just reproduced, even though in that verse that word is used specifically of mortal beings.

The 'one thing and the same' that all human mortal beings do is deal out being, the being within which each one dwells, within what Hopkins would describe as a 'cleave' of the uncloven whole of all possible worlds.[20] His analogies for this are an unsliced pomegranate and a 'burl'. A burl is a knot. It is either a knot in wood such as might demand the discernment and steady hand of a draughtsman like Hopkins to trace, or it is a knot in wool or woolly thinking the disentangling of which would require such ingenuity as is manifested by that of the philosopher whom Hopkins rated the 'rarest-veinèd unraveller'.[21]

The distinction between fact and fate is picked up later in the Comments when Hopkins returns to the notion of personality and makes clearer the traditional way adhered to by him of distinguishing the higher end of the chain of being from the lower. Where there is no question of will, he says, the doing-be and the doing-choose become mere fact. Now some facts will be states of the natural world, not least of the person's own body and the bodies of others in relation to which the human self is capable of responding freely, according to an argument outlined earlier in the Comments. This argument begins with his asking his reader to imagine three selves, *a*, *b* and *c* among whom are distributed various natural features such that *a* and *b* both exhibit A but only *c* exhibits M and not A. Imagine further, he requests, that *a* uses that shared feature well, and is saved, but *b* uses it badly and is damned. He concludes: 'Now as the difference of the facts and fates does not depend on A, which is the same for both, it must depend on *a* and *b*.' As the formula 'doing choose' suggests, the context of this argument is an argument for freedom of will. But what this argument on its own seeks to establish is that 'selves are from the first intrinsically different'.[22]

For the will to be exercised freely the self must be clad in natures sharable between different individuals that are separated one from another by unique non-general and non-specific impredicable differences. Given that stress and instress are degrees or pitches of will, and given that Duns Scotus too argues for the primordiality of will, there is good reason to give an affirmative answer to Hopkins' question, 'Is not this pitch or whatever we call it then the same as Scotus' *ecceitas*?'[23] Pitch or stress or instress, but not inscape. He and we could not call it that. And we are now in a better position to see why to the question posed in our second chapter asking whether inscape is the same as *haecceitas* the answer must be that it is definitely not. We are in a better position to see this now because, although it remains to be shown what turns on the distinction between the ways in which Hopkins spells this Latin word, we can now read the distinction between inscape and instress against the background of Hopkins' reflections on being. We may begin to wonder whether Hopkins, perhaps without fully realising it, is experimenting with the thought that in the hyphenation of being and doing inscape stands to being as instress stands to doing. Perhaps these visible or invisible hyphenations are chiasmic, hence neither synthesising nor contradictively negative nor separative, but formally distinctive in the Scotist sense to be explained in the next chapter and exemplified in the chapter following that one by the traditional doctrine of Being and the Good as distinct but really inseparable Transcendentals.

4

Hopkins' Double Discovery, of Scotus and of Himself

Two years after his conversion from High Anglicanism to Roman Catholicism Hopkins wrote in a letter dated 12 February 1868 sent from the Oratory School at Edgbaston to Alexander Baillie: 'I find myself in an even prostrate admiration of Aristotle and am of the way of thinking, so far as I know him or know about him, that he is the end-all and be-all of philosophy.'[1] A different conversion is marked in a letter dated 20 February 1875 which Hopkins addressed to Robert Bridges from Saint Beuno's College near Saint Asaph (Llanelwy) in North Wales:

> I have had no time to read even the English books about Hegel, much less the original, indeed I know almost no German. (However I think my contemporary Wallace of Balliol has been translating him.) I do not afflict myself much about my ignorance here, for I could remove it as far as I should much care to do, whenever it became advisable, hereafter, but it was with sorrow I put back Aristotle's Metaphysics in the library some time ago feeling that I could not read them now and so probably should never. After all I can, at all events a little, read Duns Scotus and I care for him more even than Aristotle and more *pace tua* than a dozen Hegels. However this is me, not you.[2]

'However this is me, not you.' On the one hand this could be a commonplace sentence used to convey the letter writer's realisation that it is time he stopped talking about himself and showed more interest, or more than interest, in the addressee. On the other hand it could sound somewhat strange. It could sound strange either because it sounds like a tautology, and therefore seems not to need saying, or it could sound strange because what it means is too deep for words. It reminds us of the poet-priest's searching paragraphs, composed five years after this letter to Bridges, on the text *Homo creatus est*. These paragraphs begin by saying that during the retreat he has been making in the summer of that year at Liverpool, 'I have been thinking about creation.' But creation is what Hopkins was thinking and writing about throughout most of his life, Divine Creation and human creations, not least creations of the artefacts produced by inventors in the field of poetry and music and architecture and other arts and crafts, not to mention, as Hopkins rarely does, the natural sciences and engineering. *Homo creator est.*

The word *homo* here may refer either to human beings in general or to a particular human being, for instance Hopkins as distinct from, say, Bridges, or to either of these individual human beings in the concrete first person singular inhabiting of his life. Hopkins begins, but only begins, to make the necessary distinctions when he writes, 'I find myself both as man and as myself something most determined and distinctive, at pitch, more distinctive and higher pitched than anything else I see.'

'I find myself.' In this finding of himself 'as man' Hopkins is telling us something about the kind of finding, not something about what is found. In particular, he is not telling us that he finds himself to be a member of the human race, a rational animal. So he is not telling us that he finds this in the way magistrates or juries find a defendant guilty, or in the way a public proclamation might be made from a throne by a sovereign or a pope. That is to say, he is not finding in the way that is in play when I say 'I hereby find . . .' Nor are we doing that at this stage of the investigations we are pursuing in this book. In them we are occupied with findings of a more private sort, empirico-phenomenological findings that Hopkins makes about himself either *qua* man or *qua* this man Gerard Manley Hopkins or *qua* the I of the bearer of that name who only on special comparatively formal occasions thinks of himself as the bearer of that name, for instance when undergoing interrogation in a law court or when applying for a passport or, he might want us to add, when answering a question posed by the holder of the keys of the Kingdom.

Findings of this sort are accompanied in Hopkins' writings by hints of the elaborate non-empirical principle of sufficient reason that Descartes inherits from his Scholastic predecessors and puts to use in one of his arguments for the existence of God. According to this principle, although when regarded as states of consciousness all ideas are equal, when functioning as representations they reflect differences of metaphysical and epistemological status. When functioning as representations ideas that stand for finite substances claim more reality 'objectively', that is to say in their capacity as representations, than those which stand for accidents or modes. Those that stand for an infinite substance lay claim to more reality as representations than do ideas of finite substances. The efficient cause of a thing must have at least as much reality as the effect has formally (actually) where cause and effect are of the same ontological category (substance or accident or mode, and so on); and if the reality of the cause is of a different category from that of the effect, it must be of a higher category or as high a category (where finite substance is of a higher category than an accident and a mode and where infinite substance is of a higher category or supercategory than that of finite substance).

This terminology of formal, objective and eminent being would have become familiar to Hopkins through the philosophical part of his training for the Jesuit priesthood. It lurks behind his defamiliarising rethinking of it undertaken both in his poetry and in such pieces of prose as are fired by the text *Homo creatus est* in his Comments on *The Spiritual Exercises of St Ignatius Loyola*. Hopkins simultaneously recreates (and decreates)[3] the Scholastico-Aristotelian categories and the Christian reanimation of Aristotle that the Schoolmen had brought about. The Comments on Loyola are not only a refreshment of those parched doctrines of ideas and causality that are defended or attacked in medieval metaphysics. They are also a gloss on that simultaneously unpuzzling and puzzling sentence in the letter cited from Bridges, 'However this is me, not you.' The combination of oddness and tautological banality that characterises this sentence is a consequence of Hopkins' aim to translate Scholastic discourse into an idiom that does justice to Scotus' idea of *haecceitas*. That process of translation is underway when, in paragraphs comparable with ones in Augustine's *Confessions* and Descartes' *Discourse on Method* and *Meditations*, he writes:

> I find myself both as man and as myself something most determined and distinctive, at pitch, more distinctive and higher pitched than anything else I see; I find myself with my pleasures and pains, my powers and my experiences, my deserts and guilt, my shame and sense of beauty, my dangers, hopes, fears, and all my fate, more important to myself than anything I see. And when I ask where does all this throng and stack of being, so rich, so distinctive, so important, come from nothing I see can answer me. And this whether I speak of human nature or of my individuality, my self-being. For human nature, being more highly pitched, selved, and distinctive than anything in the world, can have been developed, evolved, condensed, from the vastness of the world not anyhow or by the working of common powers but only by one of finer or higher pitch and determination than itself and certainly than any that elsewhere we see, for this power had to force forward the starting or stubborn elements to the one pitch required. And this is much more true when we consider the mind; when I consider my selfbeing, my consciousness and feeling of myself, that taste of myself, of *I* and *me* above and in all things, which is more distinctive than the taste of ale or alum, more distinctive than the smell of walnutleaf or camphor, and is incommunicable by any means to another man (as when I was a child I used to ask myself: What must it be to be someone else?). Nothing else in nature comes near this unspeakable stress of pitch, distinctive-

ness, and selving, this selfbeing of my own. Nothing explains it or resembles it, except so far as this, that other men to themselves have the same feeling. But this only multiplies the phenomena to be explained so far as the cases are like and do resemble. But to me there is no resemblance: searching nature I taste *self* but at one tankard, that of my own being.[4]

From the remark within parentheses and from other sentences in this 'great text' (to use again the words Hopkins uses of Parmenides' poem in praise of being),[5] it is evident that although Hopkins' ultimate topic is the incomparable and the incommunicable, the path to it passes through the minimal meta-comparison necessary to establish of two things that they are incomparable. His poems and his poetic prose are experiments that test the limits to comparability which are exposed when resemblance, likeness, identicality, difference, diversity and their literary counterparts simile, metaphor, analogy, allegory, symbol and so on are invoked in what he regards as his mission to observe and record and laud the inscapes of the world.

It is late on in the paragraphs recording the results of his observations of 'the world within' that Hopkins asks his provocative question, 'Is not this pitch or whatever we call it then the same as Scotus' *ecceitas*?' The attempt to answer this question about pitch and about thisness (*ecceitas*) should cast light on Hopkins' reference in the cited paragraphs to the determinate, the distinct, 'my individuality', 'the incommunicable', and resemblance or likeness. It may also cast light in due course on whether there might be a good reason for Hopkins' dropping of the initial 'h' with which Scotus prefers to spell the Latin word. This omission may be only a slip. However, with a philologist as punctilious as Hopkins it is more likely to be a spelling he intends. The 'good reason' just referred to will not emerge until later in this study. Here and now we turn to another puzzle raised by Scotus' word, whatever we take to be its initial letter. I refer to a perplexity raised not by the initial letter of the word in question but by its final syllable.

The -*itas* component of that word is systematically misleading. Like the 'ness' of 'thisness' and 'twoness' and like the 'ness' of the 'suchness' of 'as such', its -*itas* denotes specificity, essence, nature or kind at the meta-level either of second intentionally abstract universality or of metaphysical commonness. It is therefore exactly not a proper name for the singularity that Scotus and Hopkins are especially keen to bring to their readers' attention. The same dilemma is presented by the term *entitas* which Scotus uses of the positive entity that, he argues, is the cause of a thing's *individualitas*. Does *entitas* denote a being, an entity, or does it denote an entity's entitivity, a being's beingness? It can denote either and both: either a being of first (direct) intention or, as beingness, a being of second (indirect) intention.

What it denotes will depend on our purposes, for instance on Heidegger's when on the way to the composition of *Being and Time* he finds himself drawn to compose a treatise on Duns Scotus' theory of categories and, wrongly believing it to be another work by Scotus, on Thomas of Erfurt's theory of signification. It is not surprising that in that treatise Heidegger affirms that for Scotus 'the individual is an irreducible ultimate'.[6] That is an assertion about a certain entity, not an assertion about the entitivity of any entity what- or whomsoever; it is not an assertion about the being of any being. And here *Being and Time* itself can assist in the interpretation of Scotus. In that book Heidegger makes frequent use of the expression *Seinsweise*, which means, we noted, way or mode of being. It is an expression that makes patent the gerundial force of being which is crucial to his argument in *Being and Time*. It is crucial also in Scotus' understanding of the entitivity of the *ens*. And Hopkins is following Scotus when he insists, as we have begun to see, that the being of a being is a being-doing.

This momentous observation that the being of a being is a being-doing leaves us still with the need to find a way of signifying the individual in a manner that minimises the risk of confusing it with the thing's individuality, its *individualitas* or (in case an ultimate singular can have no such property as suchness) with its *individualitas* as such (in case the as such is other than the property of suchness, other than the property of property). The risk is that of confusing second intentionality with first intentionality, for instance – Avicenna's instance (though Frege has one that comes from the same stable) – horseness with the horse and the horse as a class with the horse as a singular member of that class. That risk is not avoided by recourse to Scotus' term *haecceitas* or to *singularitas* or 'singularity'. Perhaps it is Hopkins' alertness to the danger of this slippage that leads him to strike a compromise by opting for an alternative: *ecceitas*.[7] Although this retains a component that denotes the second-level or second-intentional nominalised abstraction -ness or -ity, the first component, *ecce*, breaks with denotation, nominalisation and constatement, replacing or supplementing the indicative *haec*, 'this', with an imperative that means 'Look'.

The speech act accomplished by this imperative is what Derrida, extending John Austin's use of the expression, would classify as performative. In Austin's use of this term a performative speech act brings into existence as a constatable nominalised fact something that is effected and made in the deed that is done in using the verb in the first person present and usually non-continuous form. For example, saying 'I (hereby) warn you . . .' is under certain circumstances enough to produce the warning as a new fact or state of affairs in the world. Retaining the Austinian conception of performativity as part of his own conception of it, Derrida includes also in his own conception of it the possibility of effecting a deed by saying something where the deed is described as, for instance, frightening someone though this deed of frightening someone is done by saying, for instance, 'I warn you'. Here the frightening that is done is a *per*locutionary effect, a deed done consequentially, contingently and extrinsically *by* saying something as distinguished from an *il*locutionary deed, a deed done *in* saying something, done thereby, where, NB, the *by* of this thereby and of its implied antecedent hereby marks a logico-rhetorically intrinsic deed, not a consequential, contingent or extrinsic one.

The performative force, whether illocutionary or perlocutionary, is practical as commonly contrasted with theoretical. It is the force of a productive, poietic or creative act as exemplified for instance by Hopkins' writing a poem the declared aim of which is to praise creation or Creation understood either as the objective correlative of a noun or as the objective correlative of a verb. Not only what we regard as poetic creation is poetic and poietic, that is to say productive. A flat prose statement can be that. Any statement is something made, an artefact, even if it makes no pretensions to being a work of art. Many of the sentences Scotus writes in prose do not for the most part display that ambition. Those in verse that Hopkins is best known for do. Some of the sentences for which he deserves to be known belong to the genre of poetic prose. Then there are his words of plain prose, words of Hopkins in his capacity of philosopher to which it is one of this book's purposes to draw attention, in line with its epigraphs.

Thus, departing (both starting and diverging) from Scotus, not the least of Hopkins' own creations is his recreation of the strange word *ecceitas* in conformity with his declaration that it is the creator's responsibility to create or celebrate 'All things counter, original, spare, strange', even 'barbarous'. Poetic creation, his manifesto stresses, should be creation of what is strange and idiosyncratic to the point that the very grammar of a particular language may be queried and queered, as for example when the verb 'to achieve' is grafted on to a noun in Hopkins' reference to the kestrel's 'achieve of' and when, in pursuit of the opportunities afforded by crossbreeding being and doing, he produces in *ecceitas* the chiasm of an imperative verb and an abstract nomination. I say that he sings of or directly sings these barbarisms partly in order to acknowledge that what cannot be said can sometimes be sung, sung of or whistled, despite the objection Frank Ramsey makes to Wittgenstein, who was an accomplished whistler, that 'What we can't say, we can't say, and we can't whistle it either.'[8] An acknowledgement must also be made of the conditional clause 'if it were good English'[9] which Hopkins attaches to his statement that in pitch, which belongs to the vocabulary of music and is, he says, ultimately simple positiveness, there might be expressed the *energeia* of the work he refers to as '*doing* be'.

The stress and instress to which Hopkins applies the term *energeia* is the *actum*, the deed, or the *actus*, the will or desire or love, that, in Scotus' terms, condenses or contracts (*contrahere, contractus, contr-actus*) to impredicable individuality the predicable patterns or designs, figures, forms or common natures to think which as natures is to perform not a contraction but an abstraction (*abstrahere, abstractus, abstr-actus*). The references made in our third chapter to judgement and to 'the foredrawing act' suggest that reading Scotus confirmed a predisposition inherent in Hopkins' writings at least as early as his comments on Parmenides, before he had discovered the writings of Scotus. It is by no means evident, however, that in his comments on Parmenides he has a firm hold on Scotus' notion of common nature. That is a metaphysical notion, a notion of something that really exists, though not necessarily in the realm of the physical. On the other hand, the notion of a common nature is not a purely logical one like that of the universality of the universal in terms of which Hopkins couches his exposition of Parmenides, for instance when he says:

> without stress we might not and could not say Blood is red but only This blood is red or The last blood I saw was red nor even that, for in later language not only universals would not be true but the copula would break down in particular judgments.[10]

A particular is a case falling under a universal. A common nature may assume the logical status of universality or numerical singleness, but in itself it is neutral in respect of universality and numerical singleness. To cite Avicenna again as cited by Scotus, horseness is just horseness. This is what is meant by saying that a common nature possesses a unity that is less than numerical, *minor unitas quam sit unitas numeralis*.[11] But this less than numerical unity is capable of combining with a posited numerically unique entity the haecceity of which inherits the metaphysical reality of the common nature. The status of the common nature is therefore not the logical status of an instantiation of a universal. The purely logical status of a universal allows a universal to have no instance. But the metaphysical status of a common nature means that it is realised in an individual which, though distinguished from the universal logically, is inseparable from the common nature in reality.

Hopkins' pages on Parmenides, composed before he read Scotus, leave in doubt whether he always recognises this distinction between the common nature and the universal. Therefore it is sometimes unclear whether he quite gets hold of what Scotus usually means by what he terms *distinctio formalis*. Some of the unclarity in what Hopkins says in connection with Parmenides derives from his failure to make explicit whether 'This blood' is short for, say, 'this drop of blood', where 'drop' is a count-noun as distinguished from 'blood' taken as a mass-noun, a name for stuff.

A formal distinction is one that lies ontologically between a real separation and a purely abstract intellectual distinction, somewhat as synthetic a priori statements, if there are any such, are logically intermediate between empirical statements and tautologies. I say 'somewhat' because these latter distinctions are logical ones, whereas a formal distinction is metaphysical in that it concerns being, which for Aristotle is the topic of the science of metaphysics. If rationality is the determination that distinguishes humanity as a species of the genus animality, what, Scotus asks, distinguishes this human being Socrates from that human being Plato, or (recalling Hopkins' 'However this is me, not you') what distinguishes this human being Hopkins from that human being Bridges? What, he asks, ultimately determines the individuality of each of these beings? He is asking not what distinguishes them conceptually or physically, but what causes and founds ontologically the impredicable numerical unity, individuality or singularity of the individual entity. Without an answer to this question, he maintains, we have no basis on which to ground the objectivity of natural, metaphysical, moral or theological science. The answer cannot be discovered in the specific nature common to, say, Socrates and Plato. For the specific common nature of a being is indifferent to the being's singular individual unity. In line with the principles of sufficient reason and eminence as explained earlier in this chapter, the cause of this individual unity must therefore be a positive individual entity whose relation to the thing's common nature is one of formal distinction therefore real inseparability. In the life of the wayfarer, pilgrim or hitch-hiker thumbing lifts on the highways of this world *ici-bas*, any matter that has to do with that causal entity is a matter that has to be accepted on faith. All Scotus can do in support of his claim is criticise alternative accounts until no further alternatives seem to be available. Hence, unless he also has an argument to show that there are no further alternatives, his argument is ad hominem or ad feminam.

The alternatives Scotus considers are as follows:[12]

(1) The *nominalist* position according to which nothing is required for material entities to be singular. They just come singularly individuated of their own accord. Against Plato the nominalists argue, with Aristotle (*Metaphysics* 1038b10–11), that the substantial being of a thing must be proper to it, not in something else.

(2) The *negationist* position defended by Henry of Ghent according to which the singular individuality of a thing is due to the twin negations

comprised of its not being another thing and its not being subdivided in the way of a heap.

(3) The *existentist* position taken up by Giles of Rome according to which a material thing owes its individuality to actual existence.

(4) The *quantitist* position, also defended by Giles, according to which quantity in size, or shape is a key to individuality.

(5) The *materialist* position according to which the singularity of a bodily 'this' is to be explained by matter.

> Against (1) Scotus adopts a realist stance analogous to what appeals to Hopkins in Platonism despite reservations he shares with Aristotle.
>
> Against (2) Scotus insists that the independent explanatory entity must be not negative, but positive.
>
> Against (3) Scotus objects that this standpoint fails to distinguish the issue of the what of a thing, its *ti estin*, from the fact that the thing is, its *hoti estin*. This is a criticism that confirms the validity of an argument we shall develop in the next chapter against the claim that Scotus himself does not make this distinction.
>
> Against (4) Scotus maintains that the quantitative predicates are accidental, and that, as maintained in the standard Scholastic version of the principle of sufficient reason paraphrased above, accidents are too weak to serve as (material, efficient, formal or final) causes of substantial individuality.
>
> Against (5) Scotus objects that it begs the question. It posits a factor that can be explanatory only if the question of what singularises has already been answered for the supposedly explanatory factor itself.

Hopkins could endorse all of these responses, but with reservations as to the fifth based on the recognition that, as the Thomist proponent of it would reply, in a metaphysical sense of matter contrasted with form and understood along Aristotelian lines as *materia prima* a material cause is not accidental but substantive.

This leaves us still in need of an answer to the questions whether the substantivity is that of a mass or that of an individual, and what the individuating cause of the undividuality of a singular thing is. Scotus and Hopkins agree that a full answer to the second of these questions exceeds the limits of finite understanding. What they say is continuous with the theological and religious reasons for not venturing beyond strict limits with positive claims to knowledge of the divine. This continuousness is what is affirmed against Thomism in Scotus' doctrine of the univocity of being. This doctrine is consistent with the doctrine that the logical and ontological function performed by what is intrinsically singular cannot be explained solely by terms that signify only common natures or universals.

The range of signification of the metaphysical common natures and of the logical universals stands in a relation of formal distinction both 'downward' with finite singulars and 'upward' with the infinite Singular of singulars. The range of signification or the reference of singularity is confined to each singular. Its singularity is, to use an adjective used by both Scotus and Hopkins, incommunicable to other entities.

Hopkins can sometimes seem to betray a passionate desire to come out with expressions that are reducible to the pattern 'This is this' or 'This is called this' or 'I am that I am' or 'I am other than you'. Of such pronouncements Wittgenstein writes that they illustrate 'a queer conception' that 'springs from a tendency to sublime the logic of our language . . . when language *goes on holiday*'.[13] 'And we can also say the word "this" *to* the object, as it were *address* (*aussprechen*, apostrophise, call up, single out by name) the object as "this" – a queer use of this word, which doubtless only occurs in doing philosophy.' He says we *can* also say this. This is possible despite the tendency of the logic of our language not to allow us to. When it does allow us to our language no longer seems to be ours. It seems instead to be foreign, barbarous. This is how the language of Hopkins' poetry sounds when instead of Latinate constructions and vocabulary he prefers earthy Anglo-Saxon or even, occasionally, Welsh ones. The very word 'Welsh' means foreign, outlandish. The language it names opens up for Hopkins the chance of a short cut to the creation of that sense of estrangement he wishes his poetry to bring about: that escape to the alternative geometry and geography of inscape where the tendency to sublime the logic of language that Wittgenstein writes of is exemplified by the situation he himself alludes to in which, he says, we imagine ourselves peeling off an appearance from the things that appear. 'It is as if we detached the colour-*impression* (*Farb*eindruck) from the object, like a membrane.'[14] It is as if we separated inseparable inscape and *instress*. It is as though we are natural realists or reists who reify nominally the adverbiality of how things appear, creating new seemings.[15]

So it is not only in doing philosophy that we allow language to go on holiday in the way Wittgenstein says that we do. We do that too in doing poetry. It is done by the philosopher-poet who writes that poetry is 'speech wholly or partially repeating some kind of figure which is over and above meaning, at least the grammatical, historical, and logical meaning', for 'some matter and meaning is essential to it but only as an element necessary to support and employ the shape [scape?] which is contemplated for its own sake'.[16] With less violence than is hinted at by these words of Hopkins', what his words say is glimpsed in what I suggest we call 'emphatically definite descriptions', expressions like '*The* mountain', '*The* village', '*The* piano' as used by a child who has not yet encountered more than one of each of these things, so does not yet distinguish common nouns from proper names.¹⁷ In such expressions the definite article is emphasised or 'stressed' and the initial letter of the noun may be written in the upper case ('The Mountain', and so on) in order to acknowledge that these titles perform a function similar to one of those performed by a proper name. They fulfil this function especially in the performance of infant baptism, but also apart from baptism at what we call a naming ceremony, when we *call* somebody or something by name and when, like the man called Adam, we are called to name it or called to rename it, as Hopkins often felt he was. This naming function is performed before the person or thing presents itself as a particular instance of a universal concept. It is in an attempt to present the world as though in its infancy that poets and other practitioners of the creative arts employ the skill that may have taken them a lifetime to acquire despite its being one that, as children, they already possessed.

Calling something by *its* name is done not when the name is a common name. Its name, ideally, will be a proper name. And where in giving something or somebody its name we aim to name something in its individuated uniqueness we would not be intending to do more than apply the proper name as a sign that points it out. Such intending is what is pointed out when instead of the expression *distinctio formalis* Avicenna employs the expression *intentio formalis*. Here *intentio* is pure reference, 'mere reference', as Charles Sanders Peirce, another admirer of Scotism, would say if reference is associated with existence.¹⁸ In the sphere of everyday speech that Hopkins took as exemplary for his poetry (if only to buck or 'buckle' everyday speech), picking something or somebody out by using a proper name like 'Tom' or an indexical expression like 'this' is usually the prelude or accompaniment to a speech act that says something about or to her, him or it. This is why in the logical grammar which all languages must possess according to Wittgenstein's *Tractatus Logico-Philosophicus* the logically proper names it posits do not work in only one way. Likewise, *intentio formalis* or *distinctio formalis* presupposes the possibility of predication prohibited in purely referential picking out, for in formal intending the metaphysical common natures in things that correspond to logical predicates in language are precisely what are contracted.

Hopkins, who not only wrote and wrote about music but also learned to play the violin, calls this process of contraction 'condensation'¹⁹ and compares it to tuning a musical instrument to a higher pitch. Decontraction, a movement in the opposite direction, would seem to be possible too. Hopkins himself is sometimes led by this possibility to speak as though 'inscape' is another term for 'instress'. A decision on whether Hopkins does or does not sometimes treat these terms as equivalents will depend on how we analyse the 'and' and the 'or' in two sentences cited above which are troublesome enough to deserve being confronted again here:

> [Parmenides'] feeling for instress, for the flush and foredrawn and for inscape is most striking . . .' and 'I have often felt . . . and felt the depth of an instress or how fast the inscape holds a thing that nothing is so pregnant and straightforward to the truth as simple *yes* and *is*.[20]

It is not evident whether the 'or' here is intended to leave open the possibility both of disjunction and conjunction. One thing that is evident, however, is that it is of a certain easily distinguished *instress*, not inscape, that he is speaking when, in another passage cited above (as early as in the first paragraph of the second chapter) he asks: 'And what is this running instress, so independent of at least the immediate scape of the thing, which unmistakeably distinguishes and individualises things?'

The reader will recall that I take the antecedent of the relative pronoun in this just cited sentence to be not 'the immediate scape' but 'this running instress', and that I take 'running' as a reference to a lapse of time in contrast to 'immediate' taken as a reference to an actual or imagined moment now, though that would be only relatively immediate insofar that the idea of an instant of time cannot be understood without an understanding of the idea of the passage of time. Moreover, as we have learned in this chapter, Scotus' distinction between common nature and individuality is a formal distinction. This means that in reality the common nature and the individuality, hence also the haecceity or ecceity that grounds that individuality, are inseparable. Hopkins' agreement with Scotus on this is tantamount to the assertion that inscape and instress are really inseparable, and that this holds also for intellect and will. Recognition of this casts a flood of light on the places at which in this chapter and the second chapter it seems as though Hopkins has not made up his mind about the distinction between inscape and instress. In some of those places his intention is unambiguous. On the other hand, if inscape and instress are really inseparable because formally distinct we should not be surprised to encounter occasions when explicit use of one of the pair of terms in question might slide into implicit or even explicit use of the other.

A further corollary of what has been said in this chapter is one that has to do with a pair of terms that figures originally in Scotus' reflections, the pair common nature and individuality. He holds that these stand in a relation of formal distinctness. Such a relation, he maintains, is one between terms that are really inseparable. By this he does not mean only that one of the terms is inseparable from the other though not vice versa. But it is only the condition of unidirectional inseparability that is satisfied in the case of metaphysical common natures that correspond to universals that have no instances, as was once believed to be the case for black swans. Is this apparent exception to the Scotian doctrine of formal distinctness removed by the consideration that common natures are metaphysical in the sense of being grounded in being? An affirmative answer to this question was given earlier in this chapter. This answer will lead to the introduction in a later chapter of the notion of near-tautology.[21] Not without bearing on what we shall say about that notion, we bring this chapter to a close by bringing together the two chief notions from Scotus that have been discussed throughout it, *haecceitas* and *distinctio formalis*, in order to ask what, precisely, is the connection between them.

So far in this chapter the first of these two notions has received much more attention than the second. But we haven't faced the question whether there are two notions here, or whether one of them denotes a part of the other. We have affirmed regarding formal distinction that it is not a theoretically conceptual or logical relation. We have noted too that it is not a relation merely between or among empirically or otherwise real entities. It is a proto-relation that lies between these realms of the intelligible and of the real. Scotus maintains that two terms are in a formal relation with each other on three necessary and sufficient conditions: they are really identical, the explanations (*rationes*) that spell them out are different, and these explanations have nothing in common. A question we have not explicitly answered is whether in a *distinctio formalis* one of the terms is a *haecceitas*. This latter is not likely to be a term directly involved in a relation of formal distinction since it is, Scotus argues, what makes individuality possible. It is an individual grounded in thisness rather than thisness itself that may with most plausibility be said to enter into such a relation. The examples of formal distinction to which Scotus gives most space have to do with the relationship of divine attributes to God, the relationship of the persons in the Trinity, and the relations of the faculties of the mind to the soul or the person. In all these cases one of the terms is an individual: God, the mind or the soul or the person. Could there be a kind of formal relation in which none of the terms is an individual? It might be useful to allow such a possibility, and I may sometimes assume that this is a possibility. But the application of formal distinction that I shall find most useful for the purposes of my application of Scotus' notion of formal distinction will work best with the cases that are standard for him. Those are the ones that enable me to rely on the entailment of existence by individuality, so they provide a basis for the 'ecological' extension I want to make of Scotus' idea to the use I make of the thought that the sheer existence of a singular entity is a good for that entity and therefore a basis for an at least prima facie responsibility towards it.

5
Some Transcendentals

The parsing of the word 'Being' attributed to Parmenides was the purpose of an essay Hopkins composed while he was an undergraduate at Oxford. The construal of that word by Scholastic metaphysicians led Heidegger to compose a dissertation under the title *Treatise on Duns Scotus' Theory of Categories and Signification* (1916). His work on that study was a factor that contributed to the strengthening of his resolve to undertake the writing of *Being and Time* in order to put in perspective the ancient onto-theological tradition for which being is a being, possibly the highest being usually called God, possibly some other being (Idea, Form, cause, will to power . . .), but always a being that conceals the 'ontological difference' between beings and being as such, a difference implicit in the ambiguity of one of the Greek terms for 'being', τὸ ὄν.

The modern tradition should not be regarded as only a historical successor to the ancient tradition. That this is not how Heidegger conceives the relation between them is confirmed by his borrowing as an epigraph for the Introduction of his *Treatise* Hegel's statement that 'with regard to the inner essence of Philosophy there are neither predecessors nor successors'. In his study supposedly of Scotus, Heidegger himself says regarding medieval philosophy that 'despite these metaphysical "inclusions" which cast light on the main tendencies of Scholasticism and which, as such, suppress or rather render impossible "phenomenological reduction", within the thinking of the Scholastic kind, and all the more markedly with it, there remain latent points of phenomenological reflection'.[1] Frederick Copleston assents to this opinion when he writes that 'Scotus' doctrine of abstract knowledge, the knowledge of essences in abstraction from existence and non-existence, has led to the comparison of this aspect of his thought with the method of the modern Phenomenological School'.[2]

Copleston's comparison is limited to Scotus' doctrine of abstract knowledge. It does not hold for the latter's doctrine of concrete intuitive knowledge of singulars as such. Nor, therefore, does it abstract from existence. If it did it would render impossible the achievement of Scotus' aim to safeguard the claim made by his realism to serve as a foundation of *scientia*. The analogy with phenomenology is nevertheless apt in so far as its subject matter is meanings or essences, as it is with phenomenology of the style practised by Edmund Husserl. But Husserl maintains that his phenomenological method draws on the capacity of the imagination to project changing scenarios with the purpose of discovering invariants. Therefore, however closely such essentialist phenomenology may match the procedures of Scotus, the latter fit less well the poetic practice of Hopkins. It may still be illuminating to describe that practice as phenomenological, but only if instead of the rigorous science of phenomenology as sought by Husserl we are thinking of something more like what John Austin and other Analytic philosophers may have had in mind when they accepted for their work the name Linguistic Phenomenology.[3] An idea appealed to by participants in this movement that is of special pertinence to an understanding of what Hopkins does is the idea of family resemblance.

As employed by Wittgenstein, the idea of family resemblance is the idea that what is meant by an expression, for instance the expression 'game' or the expression 'language', may not need to posit a semantic invariant or closed set of invariants in order for it to be understood, but only an unspecified and variable selection from an open set of possible differentia. If, instead of expecting to discover an essence understood as the content of a definition we direct our attention to one or more of the characteristics that are in different contexts possible criteria for using a given expression, we are directing our attention at – and, Hopkins might say, hoping to glimpse – a thing's inscape. Recall the reference made in Chapter 3 to the way an artist's attempt to capture a family likeness in a portrait may be frustrated by the tendency of the likeness to appear only fleetingly. The look of a face or other *motif* is a function of how the artist or viewer looks at it and its context and is struck by the likeness captured in a portrait. 'Don't think', Wittgenstein enjoins, or don't only think, 'but look'.[4] Look at the look of the face that looks back, as a poem of Hopkins would have us do, as the icon-painter, as Turner, would have us 'read' the icon and the landscape. Read Edward Thomas at the parting of the ways of which he says:

> I come home daily with pockets full of the smooth pebbles, often pearshaped (flattish), rosy or primrose coloured and transparent nearly, & in the fresh moistness wonderfully beautiful: others white & round or oval: some split & with grain like chestnuts: not one but makes me think or rather draws out a part of me beyond my thinking.[5]

Some Transcendentals

Despite the unreliability of Husserlian essentialist phenomenology as a guide to an understanding of what Hopkins may mean by 'inscape', the unreliability should not be exaggerated. Husserlian essentialist phenomenology may admit extension to the more liberal concept of meaning allowed by the idea of family resemblance. Thus the term 'essence' may be taken to mean something more flexible than it does in the lexicon of Aristotle and the Scholastics. The 'patterns' or 'designs' Hopkins calls inscapes take into account what Husserl calls *Abschattungen*, literally shadings-off or, as Hopkins would say, offshadings, aspects or sides or sidings that are marginal to or implicit in a targeted concept or percept. Hopkins would call them 'cleaves', probably in the sense both of a disjoining split (compare Greek *glyph* and German *klieben*) and in the sense of a conjoining, a cleaving together (compare German *kleben*). Therefore this 'Abelian' word[6] could be adapted in both of these senses to the distinction between categories and signification made by Scotus, and to the distinctions he makes among members of each of these domains. Categories mark off sectors of reality or meaning and hold together the entities that fall under them, preventing the doing that activates the being of these entities from being undone and scattered so that nothing is presented but nothing, 'waste space which offers nothing to the eye to foredraw or many things foredrawing away from one another'.[7]

In Heidegger's survey of these categorial and significatory domains emphasis is put on the need to attend to their historical dimensions, hence to the question of the relation of the ancient to the modern classifications just mentioned. The modern approach, as Heidegger understands it, emphasises the importance of not confusing the logical or ontological with the psychological or otherwise empirical, and of nevertheless not neglecting the connection of the logical and the ontological with the historical. This is an emphasis manifested also in the increasing importance that the historical dimensions assume in the progression of Husserl's thought from his early writings to those of the 1930s. But this emphasis is manifested too in the way Heidegger's commentary on the Pseudo-Scotus (in fact the Scotist Thomas of Erfurt)[8] begins and ends with references to Hegel. Its epigraph from Hegel has already been cited. The Hegelian note is sounded again in the many mentions of 'living spirit' made in the final paragraphs of the commentary, including its very last:

> The philosophy of living spirit, of engaged love, of union with God in reverence, toward which it has been possible to give only the most general pointers here, particularly toward a categorology demanded by its basic orientations, finds itself faced today by the considerable task of taking up a standpoint engaging the principles relating to the most powerful systematic historical perspective on the world ... and to all the fundamental motivating presuppositions of the philosophical problems raised again in his thinking by Hegel.[9]

Despite Hegel's name being the last word in Heidegger's commentary, it is not Hegel who has the last word in the conversation Heidegger has with him, for this reference to Hegel announces the history of being that Heidegger himself will outline and indeed has already anticipated in his commentary on the Scotist account of the subject matter of metaphysics, namely being, and the most common (*communissima*) notions that hold of it, namely the transcendentals unity, truth, the good . . .

Except that this ellipsis has to be shifted back a little if it is to mirror the course pursued in Heidegger's commentary. For in that commentary the Scotist theory of the good is not explicitly considered. What Heidegger tells us is that after having treated unity and truth under the heading of categories, he will treat the other transcendentals under the heading of signification. Meanwhile, to be clear from the outset about what attracts both Heidegger and Hopkins to the Scotist doctrine, we should take heed of the remark made in the Introduction of *Duns Scotus' Theory* that 'More than all the other Scholastics who preceded him he found himself with a feel for so much of what is involved in the manifoldness and exposure to tension of real life.' Scotus could well have used of himself the words 'I find myself . . .' that Hopkins will use seven centuries later to launch the quasi-confessional paragraphs of his commentary on Ignatius in which he analyses what could be referred to as, borrowing from *Being and Time*, his ownmost situatedness, his *sich befinden* or *Befindlichkeit*.

Those 'quasi-confessional' paragraphs could be described as 'quasi-*Confessional*' in recognition of the Augustinian note that resounds in them. That note is audible too in Scotus and in Husserl. The latter brings his *Cartesian Meditations* to a close by citing from Augustine's *De vera religione* the fatal words: *Noli foras ire; in te redi, in interiore homine habitat veritas*, 'Do not will to go out; go back into yourself; truth dwells in the inner man.'

The word 'feeling' in Hopkins' allusions to Parmenides' 'feeling for instress . . . and for inscape' refers not to a purely passive feeling. It refers to a competence for having a feeling, a passively active and actively passive susceptibility. The word 'feel' in the translation of Heidegger's remark about Scotus stands for '*Nähe (haecceitas)*', proximity. The word 'tension' translates '*Spannung*'. For this, readers of Hopkins might consider saying 'stress' and readers of Heidegger 'tuning'. Both of these alternatives lend themselves to interpretation in terms of the context of musical composition. This is a context akin to that of abstract mathematics for which Scotus cultivated a passion alongside the aforementioned sensitivity to the texture of everyday life. Here emerges again the duality encountered when the question arose earlier as to whether Hopkins is sufficiently aware of the difference between two concepts of contraction: on the one hand contraction towards greater individuality regarded as due to an increase in richness and depth of common nature, on the other hand contraction as a switch from the logic or metaphysics of common naturality to the logic or metaphysics of a pure individuality that cannot be separated (even by God) from common naturality but is not *in pare materia* continuous with grades of tension within a supposed scale of predicable properties and modes. The relation between these two notions of contraction is one of formal distinction.

At one place in Heidegger's study of Scotus mention of formal distinction is seized on as an opportunity to give credit to Scotus for paying heed to individuality as it is manifested in the historical. The sphere of the historical is the sphere of the 'living spirit' the importance of which we have seen Heidegger underlines in the final paragraphs of his study of Scotus. This importance is emphasised already in the book's third chapter where the identical oneness of being is contrasted with the concreteness of the historically factic and fated manifold in the context of which our thinking is advanced through analogy and metaphor and resemblance. Heidegger brings out at this stage of his reflections on Scotus or (in shudder quotes) 'Scotus', a complication that is only implicit in Hopkins. This complication results from an ambiguity in what has just been referred to as 'the identical oneness of being'. The oneness may be either numerical or less than numerical, *unitatem realem minorem unitate numerali*.[10] Heidegger regards as one of Scotus' most precious insights his contention that the unity of a common nature is less than numerical because a common nature strictly as such is capable of being expressed by different parts of speech, not only nouns, but adjectives and verbs (as is expressed in the hovering grammar of 'the achieve of' of Hopkins' kestrel). It is what is metaphysically common to the faculty of reason, to the activity of reasoning and to the characteristic of reasonability, as according to Aristotle the condition of being healthy is the core of the term used analogically of that condition of being healthy, of being conducive to health and of having a healthy complexion. In these cases health is health. As the logical and ontological point is made by Avicenna, cited by Scotus (and above), horseness is horseness. Of itself horseness is neither one nor many, neither particularity nor universality. It borrows numerical unity from that of the horse that exists in reality. It borrows plurality from horses in harness.

Heidegger applauds Scotus also for showing that Aristotle's failure to grasp fully that the fundamental unity proper to being is not numerical entails the failure of his categories to cope with future developments in the human sciences.

The ten standard Aristotelian and Scholastic categories of being are: 1. substance; then, under the subheading accident: 2. quantity, 3. quality,

4. relation, 5. action, 6. passion, 7. place, 8. time, 9. position (*situs*), 10. habitual state (*habitus*). In the first chapter of Aristotle's *Categories* references are made to naming, to definition and to grammarians. The second chapter begins with a reference to categories as parts of speech and more generally as *ta legomena*, what can or, as the case may be, cannot be said. This explains why Scotus sees the categories as preparatory for his doctrine of signification. They would be that at least indirectly even if we regarded the traditional table of categories as a systematic survey of the sectors of sensible and trans-sensible reality, as Heidegger maintains Scotus does, and as Heidegger does himself. Heidegger's survey widens until it becomes evident that he takes a chief preoccupation of Scotus to be not the distinction between the physical and the psychical or the spiritual (from which Hopkins sets out in his Comments on Ignatius), but objecthood in the most general sense. The object is a something in that it is not only related to itself but something that in being related to itself is related also to other things in not being them. 'Every thing is what it is, and not another thing' (Joseph Butler[11] – compare Hopkins: 'However this is me, not you'). The one and the other, Scotus states, are given immediately with the object: *idem et diversum sunt contraria immediata circa ens et convertibilia*.[12] Heidegger's survey widens still further to the point of suggesting that Scotus' insistence on the idea of the object reveals itself to be tantamount to Husserl's insistence that the structure of knowledge is noetic-noematic. This is Husserl's and Heidegger's 'modern' way if saying what Scotus says when he writes that *primum objectum intellectus est ens, ut commune omnibus*, 'the first object of all knowledge is an entity or entitivity (*ens*) common to everything', where knowledge of it as (an) entity (*ens*) presupposes no knowledge of it as falling under any of the accidental categories.[13] Entity (or being or primary substance) as common to every object is not a genus or class. The Scholastics call it a *transcendens*. It transcends all accidental categories. So too do the secondary transcendentals Unity (of which the numerical and less than numerical kinds were distinguished in Chapter 4), Truth, Goodness, a number of correlatives, for instance cause and caused, and a number of disjunctives, for instance finite-infinite, perfect-imperfect, actual-potential. We shall see in due course that Hopkins seems inclined to add to these Beauty, as does Alexander of Hales, who writes 'While understanding the good both as the noble (*honestum*) and the useful . . . I call the noble however what is beautiful to behold.'[14] Different from one another intensionally, the transcendentals are denotationally coextensive.

Heidegger's comments on Scotus' account of Truth as a transcendental are reminiscent of the 'veridical' conception of being Mourelatos discovers in Parmenides and of Hopkins' comments on Parmenides that treat 'to-be', 'it is' and 'there-is' as affirmations of what purports to be true or a matter of fact. Heidegger's remarks on Scotus also anticipate the former's own controversial claim that Plato's conception of truth is one according to which truth is unconcealing, *a-lētheia*.[15] A germ of this idea enters into the thought of a primitive and perhaps not quite proper sense in which truth is given with the givenness of an object as no more than simple and always 'true' representation as opposed not to falsity but to non-consciousness or non-knowledge or ignorance. Here knowledge and non-knowledge are what in his *Exploratio Philosophica* John Grote described as 'knowledge of acquaintance' and the absence of this.[16] Perhaps Bertrand Russell had read Grote and was remembering that phrase when he wrote of 'knowledge by acquaintance', contrasting it with 'knowledge by description'. I shall have it in mind when later in this book I write the word 'quaintance' because it is one that exhibits the quaintness which, at the risk of queerness, Hopkins sought to achieve with many of his coinages. The word 'quaintance' is autological in the sense that it is a word that possesses a property it connotes. Corresponding to Russell's 'knowledge by description' is what Grote calls 'knowledge of judgment'. This corresponds also to Heidegger's 'proper' sense of truth as opposed to falsity of judgement. It is truth as the correlative of knowledge understood not as acquaintance (*connaissance*) but as a knowing-that (*savoir*) which is affirmed in a complex form of words that are linked by the copula 'is' or 'are' and have a truth value (*Geltung*) rather than being merely an imitative reflection of an array of real objects. Signification – and here we are moving from categorology to signology – is the *performance* of an *act* (*actus*), where the terms here italicised should warn us that although the expression of a judgement may seem to be the making public of a private mental event, the notion of an apparently inner deed in an imagined theatre of the mind is parasitic on the logic of communications effected in the theatre of the public world. This is not the replacement of an inner world of psychic objects by an outer world of physical objects. It is a shift from this opposition towards a world where objectivity is the objectivity of logic, the so-called third realm that Frege feared the early Husserl was in danger of confusing with the realms of psychology, physiology or other fields of empirical science. Heidegger sees Duns Scotus as an anticipator of Frege and of in this respect like-minded modern philosophers such as Hermann Lotze, Emil Lask and Heinrich Rickert.[17] 'Duns Scotus', Heidegger writes, 'determines the absolute sovereignty of logical sense over all realms of knowable and known objects in speaking of the convertibility of the *ens logicum* with the objects.'[18] Scotus sees that the field of logic is the field of intentionality and that intentionality is 'expressed' (*praedicata*) via the categories of signifying judgement, so that what is analogical in the sphere of reality is univocal in the 'reduced' (*diminutus*) sphere of logic.

But if Scotus has a clear (though still loose) grip on the logic of signification, he also has a sharp eye for the empirical, notwithstanding the undeveloped nature of the empirical sciences with which he was familiar. He was therefore well equipped to avoid the 'category mistake' of psychologism. He was well equipped also to attract the acclaim of Hopkins the respecter of singularities who did not find his respect inconsistent with admiration for the Parmenides who maintained that 'The truth in thought is Being, stress, and each word is one way of acknowledging Being and each sentence by its copula *is* (or its equivalent) the utterance and assertion of it.'[19]

It is arguable even that Hopkins, with his penchant for bizarre neologism and non-standard grammar, would agree with Scotus that the traditional table of ten categories calls for supplementation by a signology whose logic of logic allows (*pace* Parmenides) a category of non-entity or unentity not admitted by the conventional table. Further, as a poet Hopkins must welcome the modification of that system of categorial sectors or 'cleaves' of reality or 'realty' by the addition to it demanded by Scotus (and Husserl and Heidegger) of privations (for instance blindness as privation of sight and Manyness as privation of Oneness or Unity) – and of poietic fictions, that is to say of things created and handmade.

On the grounds that the book by Scotus to which Heidegger devotes his treatise is concerned with theory rather than with practice Heidegger excuses himself for not treating explicitly in that treatise what Scotus has to say about transcendental Goodness. This does not mean that Heidegger's study of what Scotus writes about being, unity and truth has no implications for what Scotus writes about transcendental Goodness. One of the most interesting aspects of the traditional account of transcendentals is that each of the latter has implications for the others. Also, Heidegger himself will shortly go on to show that the superficial opposition of theory to practice is conditioned by the existential, transcategorial forms and structures described in the Analytic of Dasein of *Being and Time*.

Pragmatist or pragmaticist readings of *Being and Time* are sometimes based on an inference from the claim made in the Analytic that the theoretical stance towards things as present at hand to us in the world is a modification of the everyday stance of being in a world of what is ready or unready to hand. The world presents itself as a totality of entities when the hitherto handy becomes unhandy through becoming damaged or going missing. But whoever takes this analysis as evidence that the thesis of the primacy of practice is what is argued for in *Being and Time* (and an analogous inference is made in a popular interpretation of Bergson's *Time and Free Will*) runs the risk of paying too little heed to the distinction between primacy and primordiality, to Heidegger's insistence on the importance of equiprimordiality, and to his reminder that what he says in the Analytic of Dasein is only provisional. It is provisional in being the introduction to a more extensive phenomenological description of the structures of Dasein which are called existentials because they are structures of the ways a human being inhabits its past-ward, present-ward and future-ward temporal ec-stases. The existentialist phenomenological ontology of Dasein, Heidegger argues, should begin with the concretely existed being of the Dasein that embarks on the analysis. That is to say, as Heidegger puts it, the point at which we break into the hermeneutic circle of the *existenzial* analysis must be *existenziell*. This order of priority between the existential and the existentiel is the parallel in Heidegger's thinking to the distinction made in Descartes' thinking between the pedagogical priority of the ego and the ontological priority of God. So the phenomenology of *Dasein* must lead to a phenomenological ontology, a phenomenology of *Sein*, of being as such. This is a project that Heidegger soon ceased to describe as phenomenological or ontological.

Although Heidegger did not carry out this project, the outline and context of it just sketched says enough to make us aware of one of the most fundamental difficulties standing in the way of any attempt to read Scotus through the lens of Heidegger: Scotus conducts his arguments in the metaphysical terminology of entities and objects and subjects. Heidegger seeks to bring out in *Being and Time* that to begin with entities and objects and subjects is to begin too late. Nevertheless, this terminological difference should not rule out the possibility of discovering similarities there may be between what Heidegger is trying to do and what is done by Scotus, or indeed by Hopkins either in his prose or in his own brand of poietic thinking or thinking poietics. Something very like the mineness and mindedness each one of us experiences and enacts – what Heidegger calls *Jemeinigkeit* – is evoked in the earlier-cited paragraphs beginning 'I find myself . . .' in which Hopkins makes vivid the difference between, on the one hand, mineness and, on the other hand, the ourness of the monolithic active intellect of the Averrhoists and of the universal mind of Hegelianism:

> The universal mind being identified not only with me but also with all other minds cannot be the means of communicating what is individual in me to them nor in them to me. I have and every other has . . . my own knowledge and powers, pleasures, pains, merit, guilt, shame, dangers, fortunes, fates: we are not chargeable for one another. But these things and above all my shame, my guilt, my fate are the very things in feeling, in tasting, which I most taste that self-taste which nothing in the world can match. The universal cannot taste this taste of self as I taste it, for it is not to it, let us say to him, that the guilt or shame, the fatal consequence, the fate, comes home; either not at all or not

altogether. If not at all, then he is altogether outside of my self, my personality one may call it, my *me*.[20]

As Levinas would say, it is not the universal It or the singular Other that is first and foremost responsible. As both he and Hopkins would say, when 'I find myself . . .' I find myself guilty. That is what it means for this Jesuit champion of Franciscan Scotus to savour (*sapio*) the taste, 'more distinctive than the taste of clove or alum, the smell of walnutleaf or hart'shorn, more distinctive, more selved', tastes distinguished by bitterness, smells distinguished by acridity, yet less disgusting than 'above all my shame, my guilt, my fate'. Tastes of what both this Jesuit and this Franciscan call personality, what Heidegger calls *Dasein* and what Levinas, translating Husserl's *Beseelung*, would call *psychisme*, animation, meaning animation by the wisdom (*sapientia*) of love, though this wisdom of love would be in a chiasmic and formally distinct relationship with the love of wisdom, as, we have already begun to suspect, inscape and instress would be with each other.

Three times in the brief excerpt just reproduced the word 'fate' is heard, as, three times fate was heard knocking on the door in the excerpt selected in the section of this essay in which the word 'fate' was coupled with the word 'fact'. This is a coupling of the future and the past, the future in the past and the past in the future, in such a way that the presentness of the present is at the same time pre-sent, anticipated and 'presently' (soonly) anticipative. It is anticipative for me, Heidegger implies in *Being and Time*, of my death, but because my fate is also my shame and my guilt, it begins to look as though my being towards my death is, as Levinas maintains, less momentous and less motivating than my being towards the death of others. Equiprimordially if not simultaneously, unless we can admit a simultaneity in which my temporality is crossed by the other's temporality 'analogous' to the crossing of something said by the addressing of it, to the crossing of the constative by the performative, to the interruption of being by doing – to the *pas de deux* danced by the noun and the verb in the gerund. (A propos, of the 'gerund', from *gerundum*, thing to be done, the *Oxford English Dictionary* says that in English it is a form of the verbal noun and in Latin a verb serving as a case of the infinitive in its noun use but endowed with the versatile power to govern like their respective verbs.)

In the phenomenology of *Being and Time*, as in phenomenology generally, questions of empirically and metaphysically factual existence are suspended in favour of questions of meaning, where meaning is taken in the sense not only of the meaning of words but of meaning as the meaning of the world as lived in, hence of meaning as the transcendental presupposition of the possibility of the distinction between theory and practice, and between comprehension and comportment. Not having the advantage of a clear conception of the difference between traditional ontology and phenomenological ontology, Hopkins can get anywhere near what for Heidegger is the ontological precondition of the distinction between theory and practice only by coining expressions like 'being doing' and 'being choosing'. These expressions are enriched when they are supplemented by their being related explicitly to the good and to practice when Hopkins considers *The Spiritual Exercises* of St Ignatius Loyola. When in the course of these considerations he lists some of the powers of the finite self – which he can in the now theological context refer to as the soul understood at least as the form of the inhabited body – some of these powers will be more or less passively determined, while others will be determinative. These latter, he writes, are each 'a perfection greater than and certainly never less than, the perfection of being determined'.[21] In writing those words, Hopkins is taking advantage of the power of the word 'perfection'. This word is acknowledged also by Scotus to refer simultaneously to a theological, ontological and axiological 'property' (compare 'virtue') where the inverted commas accompanying 'property' recognise that although existence is not a ground-level property but a transcendental it is as fundamental a ground as the quasi-constative *haecceitas* and quasi-performative *ecceitas* which entail it and which, along with intention and attention, we shall find, are in a relation of formally distinctive chiasmus with each other.

In writing those words about perfection Hopkins is also giving us the opportunity to appeal to the formality of the distinction between being or existence and transcendental good in order to support the argument that the existence of a thing is a good for that thing, and that there is therefore a prima facie responsibility not to deprive that thing of that 'perfection'. In writing those words Hopkins is claiming that there is a certain equiprimordiality of theory on the one hand, and will and practice on the other hand, on a scale of theologically moral stress at one extreme of which figures free choice. Among the affirmations of this is the exercise of will in what I shall refer to variously in Chapter 11 as educated or verbal or active or positive or operative ignorance, but also, towards the end of that chapter and in the final chapter of this study, as an expression of love.

6

Another Transcendental?

Admirers of Hopkins' writings may be excused for reacting with embarrassment to the frequency with which this poet of the new and the strange so often falls back, as though at a loss for a more beautiful word, on the tired and adulterated word 'beautiful'. Surprisingly few references to the beautiful are to be found in the writings of Fransciscan Scotus, and he shows little interest in including Beauty along with Unity, Goodness, Truth and pairs like Finite-Infinite, and so on, in his list of transcendentals. One sometimes wishes that Hopkins had followed suit. Hopkins himself sometimes expressed this wish. He ached 'to give up beauty' when the beautiful began to be especially associated by him with the liturgy of the Oxford Movement that he was soon to forsake. The beautiful was therefore also associated with his Puseyite protégé Digby Mackworth Dolben who was destined soon to forsake Hopkins. Dolben suffered death by drowning at the age of nineteen. Among the poems by him that were edited by Robert Bridges, is one that begins: 'Beautiful, oh beautiful – '

John Austin pleads that, instead of spending so much time analysing the word 'beautiful', philosophers should give more attention to other words of aesthetic commendation like 'dainty' and 'dumpy'. This, he goes on to say (without pausing to wonder whether these two also are names for transcendentals), would go some way to diminishing what his philosophical contemporary John Passmore condemned as 'the dreariness of aesthetics'. Readers of Hopkins' prose may be excused in particular for wishing that he had applied his inventiveness to the search for substitutes for the b-word in some of the places where he uses it, for example where in his journal he writes:

> June 13 – A beautiful instance of inscape sided on the slide, that is successive sidings of one inscape, is seen in the behaviour of the flag flower from the shut

Another Transcendental?

bud to the full blowing: each term you can distinguish is beautiful in itself and of course if the whole 'behaviour' were gathered up and so stalled it would have a beauty of all the higher degree.

June 17 – Solar halo at sunset; it looked bigger than usual, but this was perhaps an illusion. It was of course like a rainbow incomplete.

June 19 – Two beautiful anvil clouds low on the earthline in opposite quarters, so that I stood between them.[1]

One should not expect in a personal journal the rigour one expects in a sonnet. And it is conceivable that Hopkins intended the repetitions in these journal entries to achieve one or other of the literary-cum-musical effects described in his more technical essays on prosody and in the Platonic dialogue 'On the Origin of Beauty'. The offending iteration of the word is unavoidable in this dialogue since that word names there the topic of the dialogue Hopkins imagines taking place chiefly in the garden of New College Oxford. But why does the iteration of this word offend at least me?

The *Oxford English Dictionary* says of the word 'good' that it is 'the most general adjective of commendation, implying the existence in a high, or at least satisfactory, degree of characteristic qualities which are either admirable in themselves, or useful for some purpose . . .' Of what word other than 'beautiful' could it be said that it is the most general adjective of commendation in the specific field of aesthetic sensibility? The word 'sublime'? This word may express a higher pitch of commendation, but that it is not more general than 'beautiful' is suggested by the fact that we find it more natural to say 'sublimely beautiful' than 'beautifully sublime'.[2] Or is the lesson this teaches that it is wrong to say that transcendentals are more general than other terms or that they are the most general if by that is meant that they represent genera. This seems especially wrong with the terms 'beautiful' and 'sublime'. It may also be misleading to describe these as verbal terms if the typical use of a verbal term is to describe something or refer to it.[3] Although both of these words are, in one common use of the term, 'descriptive', they are used to avoid description, to abstain from or defer predicating 'descriptive qualities'. It puts a strain on linguistic usage to say even that they are *used* if to say that is to imply that we employ and apply them for a purpose. They normally aren't called upon to serve as means. The words 'beautiful' and 'sublime' come to us unsolicited, like involuntary gasps. They are *expressions* literally pressed out, forced from us. They answer not to a felt need to represent. They answer rather to a desire not to represent, if representation is understood as speaking about – as picturing, we might say, provided in saying this we allow for the possibility that when Cézanne was working on the more than a hundred and fifty pictures he made of the Mont Sainte Victoire he was representing the mountain in the sense of *speaking for* the mountain, speaking on the mountain's behalf, for its sake (*Sache*), albeit in pigment. Hopkins too chooses a medium other than words when he draws. When he discovers himself writing the word 'beautiful' it is, as we have said, less said than sung. But for Hopkins there is no song unless there is repetition of beat. As with the word 'sublime', what the word 'beautiful' expresses is more a feeling than an idea, a feeling that reaches for an idea that we are conscious of not being able to grasp, an idea or image that is 'of course like a rainbow incomplete', like any other inscape. The very emptiness of what is full of beauty is rendered all the emptier by repetition, all the more unsuited to say more than just 'Look' or 'Listen', allowing to what we cannot describe freedom to speak for itself. It is because 'beautiful' is not descriptive but has claims to being a transcendental that for Austin to say that aesthetics should concern itself with the dumpy is to say that the subject matter of aesthetics should not be limited to the transcendental.

The case for considering Beauty as a transcendental is strengthened by its analogy with Truth and Goodness. 'Good' and 'beautiful' commend without giving much hint as to why the things they commend are commendable. And Truth is lacking in semantic content when one says that it is true that a certain thing is such and such, or exists. This is one reason why John Keats can say that beauty is truth and truth beauty, whatever we think about his right to say that this is all we know and all we need to know.

One thing readers of this book need to know is that throughout it an argument is developing which questions any such simple opposition as Aristotle might seem to endorse of, on the one hand, doing as making or producing (*poēma*) in which the doing is for the sake of the product, and, on the other hand, doing as activity (*praxis*) which is for its own sake. The latter occupies the field of the ethical, the former the realm of poetics or aesthetics. Throughout this book a defence is in course of being made for the marking out of a field I barbarously call aesthethics (*sic*). In that field, I maintain, what Aristotle says about the internal sake may hold for what he counts as external. The thought-provoking analysis of sakes that Hopkins outlines for Bridges shows that the former favours a binary analysis of sakeness. But there is good reason to recognise that a duality can be internal, as between the works of art produced and the involvement of the creator's working with the words, tones, colours or clay. That there is good reason for this recognition leaves standing the good reason for distinguishing the aesthetic goodness or badness of the work of art from the ethical goodness or badness of the artist.

Written six years before the entries just reproduced were made in his journal, Hopkins' Platonic dialogue traces the origin of beauty to a certain 'composition' described as one of likeness and unlikeness or of likeness and difference. Towards the end of the dialogue, though without mentioning his name, he touches on the idea defended by Aristotle that difference, as distinguished from diversity, presupposes a categorial likeness between the items compared (for instance two flags differ *in colour*), and that, if we take a sufficiently wide basis of comparison, each of any two items will be found to be both like and unlike the other. So that a level may be approximated to at which it becomes questionable whether two items are in a relation to each other or only one is in relation to itself. This is a possibility already implicit in the notion of repetition in so far as a repetition is a repetition of something that is the same at a different time or place. It raises the question of the validity of the principle of the identity of indiscernibles attributed to Leibniz and of the relation of what Leibniz says on this topic to Scotism.

Leibniz's metaphysics and moral theology commit him to an acceptance of the principle that without a differentiating property by which the putative duality of entities may be recognised the duality is only apparent. Leibniz's ontology defines entities in terms of ideal aspects, and only in terms of the latter could the Good Lord know which world would be the best possible to create. Therefore in his early writings Leibniz rejects Scotus' principle of individuality according to which individuality is not determined by mental or logical factors but by *haecceitas* and the will of God which is free in the sense, to be amplified below, that it is possible for Him either to will X or to will not-X or to not will either. In the *De Principio Individui* Leibniz maintains that 'every individual is individuated in its entire being', including in that being what Scotus calls common nature. 'But', one commentator on Leibniz writes, 'in his later thought individuation occurs in the individual concept or law, and his position may therefore be considered a modern version of the Scotist one.'[4] We shall see[5] that this way of describing Leibniz's development vis-à-vis Scotus, with the emphasis it puts on law and conceptuality, anticipates Peirces' response to the latter. It is not premature to draw attention immediately, however, to the power of Scotus' thesis that indiscernibles are not necessarily identical, and to the relevance of that thesis to Hopkins' almost obsessional repetition for instance of the b-word. The more a word or anything else is repeated, the higher is the chance for it to dawn upon us that likeness is not inimical to the numerical singularity of the like entities compared, and the greater is the opportunity to, in the epistemological, ontological and cosmogonic senses of the word, 'realise' the world and celebrate the increase of beings in it facilitated according to the principle of the non-identity of indiscernibles subscribed to by Scotus and endorsed by Hopkins.

The possibility referred to at the end of the last-but-one paragraph (the possibility 'already implicit in the notion of repetition') is illustrated by the remembering of phenomena, for instance the remembering on which turns the anecdote recounted in the first paragraph of our second chapter. It is also illustrated by the formal distinction between nature or essence and the haecceity of individuation. Long before Hopkins had recognised a kindred spirit in his thirteenth-century predecessor at Oxford, Duns Scotus, and while still an undergraduate there watched over by Benjamin Jowett at Balliol and Walter Pater at Brasenose, he reveals in his Platonic dialogue 'On the Origin of Beauty' that he was already armed with some of the key words he will use to formulate his more mature thoughts, for instance 'shape', 'pitch', 'emphasis', 'intensity'.[6]

These terms and the topics of metre, rhythm and rhyme discussed in the dialogue are taken predominantly from the sphere of music and poetry, confirming Hopkins' agreement with Walter Pater's dictum that 'All art constantly aspires towards the condition of music.' This does not mean simply that art has to do only with form as opposed to meaning or content. Although, in his conception of poetry, Hopkins underlines the importance of form and shape, he concedes that these are not separable from all subject matter. The participants in his imaginary Platonic dialogue agree that one of the sources of beauty is the juxtaposition of likeness and unlikeness and that implicit in this is the possibility that meanings or ideas as such can be taken as related to one another formally. Semantic and logical relations such as synonymy, antithesis and entailment have their own inscape, that is to say, their pattern or design.

Hopkins' frequent use of these words 'pattern' and 'design', combined with his reference in the dialogue to the relation among parts and to the whole as an origin of beauty, will lead some of his readers to conclude that his account of that origin includes the traditional argument from design to the existence of God. But that is not how the notion of design fits into his own thinking. At no stage does his thinking or, to cite Edward Thomas again, something 'beyond his thinking' about design seem to depend on or argue towards the existence of a divine Designer. The need for such an argument appears never to arise with him. It is rendered unnecessary and irrelevant by his having always already found himself in love with the inscapes of the world and by his identification of these with the Incarnation which, in the wake of Scotus, he regards not as a reparation for human sin but as a way of manifesting the love which the Creator also manifested in His contingent choice of this world over other possible ones.[7] For Hopkins the existence of a divine Creator is an absolute presupposition, that is to say unquestioned, not a proposition for the truth of which arguments have to be produced. His conviction is signalled not by a probative *ergo* but by a disclosive *ecce* without which even the *ergo* of the argument to a first cause is incomplete.

However, the existence of a divine Creator will not be an absolute presupposition for many readers who yet remain interested in obtaining an account of the origin of beauty. The theist may maintain that untheistic readers will be able to obtain a true account of the origin of beauty only via conversion to theism. But to maintain that is to raise the methodological difficulties attached to the *via negativa* and to a certain closely related manner of proceding that I call 'educated ignorance' and will describe in the penultimate chapter of this essay.

In the paragraphs of the Comments on Loyola in which Hopkins describes the self-taste which is both the transitive verbal means and the intransitive nominal end of his self-finding, he juxtaposes 'my shame' and 'sense of beauty'. Is that because his sense of the beauty of the created inscapes of this world is a ground for his shame and a reason for him, soon after he joined the Jesuit novitiate in 1867, to make a holocaust of his poems? And wouldn't doing that be one way of imitating the Christ whose name rhymes with 'sacrificed'? If Hopkins endorses Scotus' teaching that being is univocal and if beauty is a transcendental, it would be natural for Hopkins to think of the scale of being as a scale of beauty of which a lower degree should be sacrificed for a higher degree of perfection. Supported by Hopkins' sermons 'On Personality, Grace and Free Will' and 'Creation and Redemption: The Great Sacrifice', Christopher Devlin observes that for Hopkins Christ is the first beauty, *prima species primaque pulchritudo*.[8] It is worthy of notice that the word *species* in this phrase, as well as being a possible synonym for 'beauty', translates 'pattern' in the sense both of design, hence inscape, and image or paradigm or diagram or exemplar. It also deserves notice that readiness to sacrifice oneself is a requirement of truly agapeistic love. So it is arguable that the scale of increasing beauty is a scale of increasing love.

Hopkins' recourse to the words 'beauty' and 'beautiful' is so frequent that he courts the danger of diminishing the chances of their working at full pitch. An illustration of his over-use of them was cited above from his journal. In one of his poems, 'The Leaden Echo', he asks

> How to kéep [. . .]
> Back beauty, keep it, beauty, beauty, beauty . . . from vanishing away?

In 'The Golden Echo', he enjoins

> Give beauty back, beauty, beauty, beauty, back to God, beauty's self and beauty's giver.

Despite the equation here of the b-word and the G-word, and despite the repetition of it here and in two other places in the same poem, which is hardly more than a single page long, something happens that begins to make up for what to my ear the b-word lacks. The lack (*carentia*) is the disappointment of finite beauty exemplified in French equivalents of the adjectival mutation of the word as it occurs in the phrases *beaux arts* and *belles lettres*. These phrases imply a context in which, no matter how high a degree of accomplishment the work of literary or other art in question may attain, the context itself implies in turn an objective detachment from matters that are more urgent because they affect the welfare of others rather than being cultivated only for one's own pleasure. It is not merely the incult philistine who regards the beautiful in this way. This is how the beautiful may be regarded by anyone with moderately sensitive antennae. The institutionalising of the aesthetic implied in these two French phrases is a corollary of the intersubjectivising endorsement Kant and others hold to be expected by anyone who says of a thing that it is beautiful.

Despite his admiration for Turner and Ruskin, Hopkins did not write a Platonic dialogue on the origin of sublimity. Had he done so, he might have said whether he shared Ruskin's belief that 'it will be found that the highest beauty is sublime, and the highest Sublimity beautiful, and yet the Beautiful and Sublime are totally distinct ideas . . .'[9] Had he done so, he might have said too whether he believed that this distinction is one aspect of the chiasmic jointure of connotative similarity or dissimilarity and real denotative individuality that Scotus names *distinctio formalis*. We can only guess that Hopkins took this view. We can only guess too whether he saw beauty and sublimity as incongruent counterparts on analogy with the thought experiment in which Kant invites us to try to superimpose or to imagine one glove of a pair superimposed on the other without its being turned inside out.[10] This cannot be done in Euclidean space despite the fact that the description of one of the gloves in the relationalist conception of geometry favoured by Leibniz is identical with the description of the other.

In what may be called the aesthethical turn, and reminding us that according to Kant the sublime and the moral overlap each other, there takes place a volte-face from self-affection to affection by another, whether that other be non-human, another human being like ourselves, Christ or 'beauty's self and beauty's giver', as though for Hopkins the b-word is synonymous with the G-word, and as though the aesthetical turning is an ethical turning and a religious turning in a fundamentally oecumenical sense of the word 're-lig-ious' that does not imply an institutionalised religion or Deity. This is what we should expect if we admit beauty to the family of transcendentals and define the latter, among them the beautiful and the good, as coextensives. Hopkins himself gives us a word for this turning when, still in 'The Golden Echo', he gives us the word 'loveliness'. This is a better word than 'beauty', or a word for a better beauty. As 'The Windhover', dedicated to Christ *and* our Lord, may be interpreted as saying, 'beauty . . . is a billion times told lovelier' by this word 'lovelier' because 'loveliness' is a noun with a verb dancing at its centre, like Parmenides' word 'Being' in the exegesis of it given by Hopkins, and like George Herbert's word 'Love' as it works in the poem of which it is the title:

> Love bade me welcome: yet my soul drew back,
>   Guilty of dust and sin.
> But quick-ey'd Love, observing me grow slack
>   From my first entrance in,
> Drew nearer to me, sweetly questioning,
>   If I lack'd any thing.
>
> 'A guest', I answer'd, 'worthy to be here':
>   Love said, 'You shall be he.'
> 'I, the unkind, the ungrateful? ah my dear,
>   I cannot look on thee.'
> Love took my hand and smiling did reply,
>   'Who made the eyes but I?'
>
> 'Truth, Lord, but I have marr'd them; let my shame
>   Go where it doth deserve.'
> 'And know you not,' says Love, 'who bore the blame?'
>   'My dear, then I will serve.'
> 'You must sit down,' says Love, 'and taste my meat.'
>   So I did sit and eat.

What Love says is 'Love', with the imperativity of 'Love thy neighbour' to be heard in Hopkins' poem or prayer beginning 'Thee, God, I come from, to thee go' the simplicities and inversions of which are reminiscent of Scottish metrical psalms and perhaps of the 'more balanced and Miltonic style' to which in a letter to Bridges Hopkins admitted he aspired.

> I have life before me still
> And thy purpose to fulfil;
> Yea a debt to pay thee yet:
> Help me, sir, and so I will.
>
> But thou bidst, and just thou art,
> Me show mercy from my heart
> Towards my brother, every other
> Man my mate and counterpart.

The formal respect towards God expressed by the vocative 'sir' in the first of these verses is also a respect towards the human. Its mode of address is that of the vocative 'Lord' in Herbert's poem. The two words hover over the distinction between the human and the divine as I do when I draw attention to the rule which that poem introduces to legitimate the replacement of the G-word by the word 'Love'. That that rule, Herbert's rule, is Hopkins' rule is made plain by the latter's remark: 'All things therefore are charged with love, are charged with God and if we knew how to track them give off sparks and take fire, yield drops and flow, ring and tell of him.'[11] Once the translation rule is given, and provided it is kept in mind, I can, suspending disbelief, use it to backtranslate from agapology to theology as in these recent paragraphs I have done without inhibition in order to recognise how Hopkins sees a way to keep beauty from vanishing away.

The transition from the first to the second of the two quatrains just reproduced goes in the opposite direction, from theology to agapology. But, guided by the poem that asks 'To What Serves Mortal Beauty?', hear and look at what happens when the human love declared in the second verse becomes one with the acknowledgement of the debt to God made in the first:

> To man, that needs would worship block or barren stone,
> Our law says: Love what are love's worthiest, were all known;
> World's loveliest – men's selves. Self flashes off frame and face.
> What do then? how meet beauty? Merely meet it; own,
> Home at heart, heaven's sweet gift; then leave, let that alone.
> Yea, wish that though, wish all, God's better beauty, grace.[12]

Merely meet merely earthly beauty and the beauty of the human being, which is the most lovable being to be met in the world. Then turn your attention in another direction, turn it to the better beauty of God, which is grace.

Grace is for Hopkins one place at which we can at least know that we must opt for willed ignorance educated by love. The education may advance far enough for us to begin to learn why we cannot learn more. In the way but also on the way of advance to further knowledge is the difficulty surrounding the use Hopkins makes in his poem of the word 'own'. This can mean owning up. It can also mean ownership, for instance in the relationship between 'men's selves' referred to by the words 'this is me, not you' of the sentence of the letter in which Hopkins' tells Bridges that he has returned Aristotle's *Metaphysics* to the library shelves in order to devote himself to reading the work by Duns Scotus that he has lately discovered. The 'own' may mean, however, not the ourness shared among human beings according to 'Our law'. It may mean the ourness in which natural or conventional human legality is subsumed under God's justice and love.

Another Transcendental?

Justice *and* love. Not just justice *or* love? Not if by justice is meant the singular plurality and verb-nominality of the lines reproduced in Hopkins' sonnet 'As kingfishers catch fire':

> . . . the just man justices;
> Kéeps gráce: thát all his goings graces;
> Acts in God's eye what in God's eye he is –
> Christ –

The just man keeps grace. So grace is not appropriated to himself by God. It is not limited only to the eye of the Beholder to whom men and women are indebted for their creation and for the creation of the kingfishers, the dragonflies and the Heraclitean fire they catch and draw. Grace in man is not just a seeming to God's eye, because in God's eye he is . . . Is what or is who? The questioner is held in suspense until at the beginning of a new line and followed by a moment of silent incredulity, the answer is given in the single and singular word 'Christ – '. Single, singular – and plural,

> . . . for Christ plays in ten thousand places,
> Lovely in limbs, and lovely in eyes not his
> To the Father through the features of men's faces.

The three-in-one-and-one-in-three increases to a one in three million and more. The Trinity grows to at least a trillionity. These last words of the poem seem to say that Christ, the Word, plays not only as one who plays in all those places, but as one who plays through the very faces, visible to God, of the human beings who occupy those places.

These three lines of the poem run parallel with the three lines of the Comments on *The Spiritual Exercises* of St Ignatius Loyola which say: 'It is as if a man said: That is Christ playing at me and me playing at Christ, only that it is no play but truth; That is Christ *being me* and me being Christ' (Hopkins' emphasis),[13] a sort of identity denied to the sender and recipient of that often-cited letter in which Hopkins says to Bridges 'this is me, not you'. The sentence just cited from the Comments occurs in the middle of a discussion of divine grace where much of what is said must be a matter of speculation or faith, for instance what is said when Hopkins says of divine grace that it is an action of the Creator that carries the creature towards the sacrifice of itself to God in which consists its salvation. He refers to this divine action as 'holy spirit'. 'Spiration', *spiratio*, he could have said following the philosopher who had lived on the Oxford air seven centuries before him. He refers to this divine action also as 'divine stress', casting light on what was said earlier in the pages of this study that treat instress and inscape, giving us to understand that in these, most directly in instress, we were treating of will.

Hopkins writes that will as natural sense of affection (*voluntas*, love, Love) is, at different stages in its operation desire, wish, enjoyment and gladness. Will as opting to act (*arbitrium*) is, before the act, purpose or determination, resolution, decision, or intention. At the time of action it is consent, avowal, or willingness. After the action it is avowal, or ratification. But here, he warns, as he warns after giving his suggestions of names for the prior stage and as he warns so frequently elsewhere in his prose writings, there is no proper word.[14] Sometimes he uses formulae like the throw-away 'whatever its name' as when in a paraphrase of Loyola's analysis of action he writes: '. . . all voluntary exercise of faculties is in such a case practical; it is not mere speculation, whatever its name'.[15] Compare 'whatever we call it' in that ground-breaking rhetorical question 'Is not this pitch or whatever we call it then the same as Scotus' *ecceitas*?' where the task of coming up with the right name for it is left to the reader.

In taking up that task I nevertheless follow closely on the poet's own suggestion, in conformity with Scotus, that the affective and the active forms of the will are correlative forms of one and the same power. The relation of these forms to that power is one of formal distinction in the Scotist sense that the relata are on the one hand definitely distinct from each other but on the other hand not separable in reality. Distinct, but not through some operation of reason only. Distinct rather *a parte rei*, in things ontologically, where 'things' covers physical and metaphysical 'realty' (*sic*). This last is Hopkins' word, but although *res* is included by some Scholastics in their list of transcendentals, it is not so included by Scotus, any more than is the *splendor formae* Hopkins refers to as beauty.

Scotus too writes occasionally about beauty. What's more, he does so in order to make clearer what he writes about goodness and duty. He is an ally in the campaign mentioned above to make sense of the notion of a science or art that could be called aesthethics (with two occurrences of the letter 'h'). Analysing the way the understanding informs the will in deciding what one is morally obliged to do, and, it should be added, in choosing hypotheses in doing natural science (both entail the manipulation of Ockham's Razor), Scotus underlines the part played by the sense of beauty in the making of moral decisions. In the words of two commentators on Scotus:

> Against the background of the foundational moral principle, *Deus diligendus est*, Scotus presents the determination of moral goodness as essentially an act of aesthetic rational judgment in the contingent order. The morally good act is, he states, a beautiful whole comprised of several elements within an appropriate relationship to one another and all under the direction of right reasoning.[16]

In the words of Scotus himself:

One could say that just as beauty is not some absolute quality in a beautiful body, but a combination of all that is in harmony with such a body (such as size, figure, and color), and a combination of all aspects (that pertain to all that is agreeable to such a body and in harmony with one another), so the moral goodness of an act is a kind of decor it has, including a combination of due proportion to all to which it should be proportioned (such as the potency, the object, the end, the time, the place, the manner), and this especially as right reason dictates should pertain to the act, so that we should say of all these things that it is their conformity to right reason that is essential.[17]

We could say that for Scotus *praxis* is related by formal distinction to *poiesis*, and that both are inseparable from music, so that when in defining formal distinction he moves from less than numerical unity to numerical unity – number – he moves to metre, to measure and to music, which Hopkins takes as his model for poetry.

In recent times the spell of Scotus has been experienced by philosophers aiming to produce a defence of the possibility of natural science that does not rest upon the metaphysical premises and principles of metaphysical science as understood by Scotus. Natural sciences of some sorts have an observational aspect and a generalising aspect. The generalising aspect is at the heart of the application of Scotism to natural science made by Charles Sanders Peirce. How that application is made will be the subject of the next-but-one chapter of this study. That chapter will now be approached, however, by one in which some further distinctions are made among the observations of a writer whose work is largely limited to the preliminary stage of science concerned with the collecting of evidence. One reason for choosing to attend to this writer is that his manner of writing up his findings seems to me to resemble the way Hopkins writes up his. Two more reasons, one of them an unresemblance, will be given in the next chapter.

The author in question, John Alec Baker, like Gerard Manley Hopkins, works in that zone of human experience in which a chiasmus takes place between poetry and science, and in which the subject matter of the science regarded as knowledge has superimposed upon it a science of seemings, where by 'seeming' (which is cognate with 'same') is meant not simply what is contrasted epistemologically with being, but also how the seemings appear in their own right phenomenologically – or phenomenographically, for in Hopkins' case the seemings are described not only through words but also, in more than one sense of the word, through drawings.

Part II

7
Seeming, Observing and Observance

Revealing, concealing, seeming, appearing, glimpsing and suddenness are topics that ask for further thought when from Hopkins, an author who crosses to and fro over the threshold between literature and philosophical theology, we turn to one who crosses back and forth over the threshold between literature and natural science.

It would be wrong to suppose that the incompleteness we have come to regard as intrinsic to what Hopkins calls inscape can be equated with the incompleteness philosophical phenomenologists like Edmund Husserl attribute to what they call *Abschattungen*. This term, sometimes translated as 'shadings' or 'offshadings' or 'slants', is introduced by these philosophers to refer to aspects of things that are not currently fully present in perceptual experience but only implied, such aspects as that of the underside of a plate resting on a table viewed from above. Although Hopkins' word 'siding' might seem to be equivalent to 'aspect', shadings are what philosophers of the British empiricist and phenomenalist tradition would refer to as possible perceptions. The hidden underside of the plate belongs to the notion of the plate's solidity. The inscape, which is more or less elusive and always changing, is, we have seen, the 'personality' of something, including the 'personality' of things that are usually contrasted with persons. This is closer to what classical medieval philosophy stemming from Aristotle calls essence, except that essence is what is given in a definition employing common nouns and universal predicates, whereas the inscape is sensorily 'glimpsed' or otherwise 'sensed'. Here 'sensing' implies more guesswork than what Husserl calls protensions, meaning by this the proleptic reference to incipient shadings or aspects. What is 'sensed', we could say, taking the hints from John Grote and Bertrand Russell noted earlier, is that with which we have 'quaintance', keeping the allusion 'quaint' makes to the singular strangeness, idiosyncraticness and 'peculiarity' to which Hopkins believes himself duty-bound as poet to give voice. What is 'sensed' takes us more or less by surprise. It does not belong simply to the sphere of verifiable possible perception constitutive of the nature or essence of a thing. It belongs typically to the sphere of the aesthetic in the sense of what is sensory or felt (the sphere of *aesthesis* surveyed, for example, in Kant's first *Critique*). It belongs also to the more special field of meaning (the field surveyed, for example, in Kant's third *Critique*) in which the word invokes skills cultivated typically though not exclusively by the artist. However, the person gifted with these artistic skills may also be a scientist. He may be a scientist seeking to establish a general law in what Kant calls reflective judgement. He may be a scientist seeking to disestablish a general law in what Kant calls determinant judgement. He may be a scientist seeking to do both of these things.

One such artist-scientist is John Alec Baker. Not formally employed as a scientist, Baker nevertheless exercised the scientific attitude for much of the sixty years of his residence in Essex, especially the ten during which he made sorties on foot or by bicycle into the countryside surrounding Chelmsford observing wildlife, above all the way of life of the peregrine. In the introduction to *The Peregrine*, Baker's record of his sightings, Mark Cocker writes: 'He acquired intimate insight into the personalities of individual birds and over the years he built up an understanding of where they would be and when.' 'Intimate insight', 'personalities', 'individual birds'. These are all expressions of the kind we have used in the course of our interpretation so far of the writings of Hopkins. It is no wonder therefore that we now find ourselves reading him through the magnifying prisms of Baker. We could say that Baker is describing the inscapes of the peregrine as Hopkins in the best known of his poems is describing the inscapes of the kestrel. We could say that the poet-priest is describing what the bird-watcher calls the 'jizz' of the bird, its attitude, *Gestalt*, disposition, stance or 'sit', when in that poem Hopkins writes

> of daylight's dauphin, dapple-dawn-drawn Falcon, in his riding
> Of the rolling level underneath him steady air, and striding
> High there, how he hung upon the rein of a wimpling wing
> In his ecstasy! then off, off forth on swing . . .

He says 'on swing', omitting the indefinite article, for it is of a definite, individual piece of 'behaviour' that the poet here writes. The poet says too that he 'caught' the view he is describing, as though the view were one 'snapped' by a camera.

Baker was more than an amateur bird-watcher. His observations, usually made through lenses of binoculars or a telescope, and his descriptions of 'scapes' are detailed. But, as Baker himself remarks on the first page of his book, 'Detailed descriptions of landscape are tedious.' When he makes this remark the reader will just have encountered the author's first use of a sentence in *The Peregrine* constructed around the word 'like': 'The plain is like an estuary of land.' This is the first of several hundred such constructions with 'like' to be met in the book. Mention of this is relevant to the risk of tedium to which the author refers, for these comparative sentences with 'like' can be means to a reduction of this risk. They can be the moment when poetry and the poetic imagination enter science, or are discovered inside it already. They can be the moment of magic in science, the Aha moment, as we used to say, the Wow moment, as we say now, the Now moment, such as when, as though for the first and last time, Dennis Potter experienced the superlativity of the blossom of the plumtree that 'looks like apple blossom but it's white'. Who would deny that the comparison recorded in Baker's 'like' sentence marks a moment at which a flash of insight comes to pass? Baker has been talking about the estuarial body of water east of his home where the rivers turn south and, ahoy, we are invited to see the land mass as a body of water. This reversal happens all of a sudden. The suddenness, mentioned in our earlier discussion of inscape, is adverbial to the shunt effected by the prepositions of comparison 'like' and 'unlike' in the work of characterising what Scotus would call a common nature.

As I have hinted (and everything turns here on hints), such a switch may be treated as a literary or otherwise aesthetic phenomenon. In those fields of experience such reorientations are valued for their own sakes, whereas in the realm of scientific thinking and experiment change of aspect is in service to increase in knowledge. The knowledge aimed at in science is normally knowledge facilitated by an explanatory theory or model, but such knowledge is more or less directly based upon or triggered by repeated or repeatable observations such as those of the peregrine made by Baker and recorded by him in language so inventive yet at the same time so faithful to what it is describing that each repetition comes across as the announcement of a singular event reported for the very first time. 'I saw my first peregrine on a December day at the estuary ten years ago', he tells us in the chapter of his book titled 'Beginnings'. That is a report of a first time, but not necessarily a report of something experienced *as though* for the first time, as, in the sense of Scotus and Hopkins, an uniquely individual *(h)ecceitas*. Two paragraphs later he repeats, 'This was my first peregrine.' Then,

> I have seen many since then, but none has excelled it for speed and fire of spirit. For ten years I spent all my winters searching for that restless brilliance,

for the sudden passion and violence that peregrines flush from the sky. For ten years I have been looking upward for that cloud-biting anchor shape, that crossbow flinging through the air.[1]

To what or to whom does this 'sudden passion and violence' belong? Is it the crossbow that flings or is it the bird that flings itself? Or is it both? For, note well, here the bird is said to be a crossbow, not just like one. Then there is 'flush', a word of which Hopkins is fond, used here by Baker to convey the thought that the sudden passion and violence are as it were washed down by rain from the sky upon the searcher beneath. Baker is not simply describing an objective matter of fact over against him. He is testifying to and vouching for an interrelationship in which he is participating. Meanwhile the searcher waits and waits, utterly bored. But

> When the hawk is found, the hunter can look lovingly back at all the tedium and misery of searching and waiting that went before. All is transfigured, as though the broken columns of a ruined temple had suddenly resumed their ancient splendour.[2]

The 'as though' proposed here is not of the kind you'd expect in a documentary catalogue of matters of fact. And that is not what Baker gives us. Nor does he give us a transfiguration with an uppercase T, as Hopkins might have, along with allusions to seeing through a glass darkly. Furthermore, the temple of which Baker writes is a pagan one. He writes also on the same page:

> In my diary of a single winter I have tried to preserve a unity, binding together the bird, the watcher, and the place that holds them both. Everything I describe took place while I was watching it, but I do not believe that honest observation is enough. The emotions and behaviour of the watcher are also facts, and they must be truthfully recorded.[3]

To speak in this way of truthful, honest and faithful records both of what is watched and of the 'jizz' of the watcher is, however, still to regard these records as representing how things are as distinguished from how things seem. Baker himself speaks of them in this second way at many places in *The Peregrine*, *The Hill of Summer* and the diaries in which he writes of how something he is describing appears, seems or looks. Those are the places where he uses the language of seeming in order to signal that he is not confident enough to claim for his observations the status of knowledge. Those are the places where what is said is cast in terms of an epistemological contrast between what seems to be and what is, between appearance and reality or, as Hopkins would say, realty. However, there are many other places in Baker's notebooks where this familiar contrast between being and seeming to be is not his main concern, places where the language of seeming is employed with a purpose that cannot be reduced to that of avoiding the greater commitment implied by employing the language of what is the case – Parmenides' language of veritative being. From among the vast number of examples of uses of the language of seeming to be encountered in his writings I shall reproduce a couple of examples of the unfamiliar kind where Baker's purpose is not obviously epistemological in the manner just explained. These examples of what seems to me a more special use of the language of seeming are taken both from *The Peregrine* and from *The Hill of Summer*, Baker's second book (but bound with the first in the edition I am using). In the latter his recourse to that language is more frequent than it is in the other one where more use is made instead of sentences using the word 'like' to make comparisons. This means that in place of sentences beginning 'It seems to me' or ones in which the grammatical subject is 'I' we tend to find ones in which the subject of the sentence refers to the thing that the sentence is about. This is to be expected in a book like *The Peregrine* where, in its second chapter for instance, the author is readier to formulate general conclusions about the bird, going as far as to draw up statistical tables supported by and supporting these findings.

I am aware of the possibility that what I take to be a special use is special to estuarian English, understanding by that the English spoken in the part of Essex in which Baker lived most of his life. I have not found evidence in dictionaries or in literary remains like *The Battle of Maldon* to confirm this possibility. Even if it could be confirmed – confirmed, say, that the to me curious character of the idiom is due to its derivation from a manner of speaking left behind in East Anglia by the Danes – it would still be relevant to consider what the force of the idiom might be.

Here is one illustration of what gives me pause:

> I watch the evening light withdraw. The estuary sinks lower as the tide ebbs away and the bland mud rises. Curlew, redshank, and grey plover, are feeding on the shore. Their subdued plaintive calls seem to fly softly, endlessly outward over the reflections of the sky in the wet mud.[4]

The import of the last sentence would be misgauged if we read the words as an expression of a cautious reluctance to affirm a simple statement of fact. What sort of fact could that be which is affirmed as the fact that the plaintive calls actually do fly softly, endlessly outward over the reflections of the sky in the wet mud? The straight opposition of being and seeming on which such an interpretation of the words would turn cannot bear the weight the author seems to me to intend. To suppose that it could would be like supposing that the effect made on us by the sound of a train receding from us as we stand on a railway bridge could be no more than the physical

Doppler effect. To suppose that would be to leave out the possibility of a non-physical emotional effect of that effect.

Again, consider:

> The bird is so large, so slow to anger, so much further back in time. It seems to have a long way to come within its own body before it begins to fall towards its prey.[5]

Is not 'It seems to have a long way to come ...' too speculative and thought-provoking to be interpreted simply as a statement of a matter of fact?

Unsimple too is:

> The detail of their plumage was difficult to see, but their moustachial bars seemed as prominent at a distance as they did when close.[6]

This is intermediate in force between the sense of seeming and the sense of being. Readers might well ask themselves whether 'were' would have been more natural, their unsureness turning on the ambivalence of 'prominent' between meaning a physical feature of the bird itself, which dictates 'seeming', and on the other hand meaning how the bird appears to the observer, that is to say on the appearance as such, not the thing as such.

This sort of ambivalence does not arise with:

> The green of the grass intensifies, then fades to grey. All shapes recede, then seem to come slowly nearer, as dusk deepens and day ends.[7]

Nor, one might think, should this ambivalence arise with

> The water seems to lose its pearly shine as it comes closer to the top of the sea-wall.[8]

Is this about the impression the water makes on us, or is it about the cause of that impression? It is about both, rather as in the language invented by Hopkins inscape is conjured by instress. Similarly with

> The view from the gate, beside the wood and past the house, seemed wonderful.[9]

Do not the concepts of view and of the wonderful ordinarily imply that the view ('Look') *was* wonderful? (Similarly for the expression of the experience of the beautiful investigated by us in an earlier chapter. When I say a view is beautiful, can I be wrong?) One cannot simply *cancel* the wonderfulness of the impression or the impression of the wonderfulness, not at least if to say that something is wonderful is to express one's admiration of it or to say that the thing is full of wonders, replete with ingenious and surprising though not necessarily namable qualities, somewhat as Baker's pages exhibit such a variety of sentences cast in the language of seeming that we can appreciate their richness and scope only if we enlarge our collection beyond the few cited so far.

In carrying out this enlargement we need to be aware that under certain conditions the function of a sentence that affirms a seeming can be performed by a sentence affirming a seeing. *How* a thing looks can become hypostasised as *what* is looked at, but without becoming identified with the epistemic object perceived. In these circumstances the 'inner', 'representative' object lends itself to being spoken of as something that is seen, though we may want to shudder-quote the second of these words as a warning that it means roughly the same as 'image' or 'picture' or 'diagram' or 'design'. The inverted commas around these last words may themselves function as shudder-quotes with readers who wish not to be misled by what they consider to be the dangers of seeing seeing or seeming as the viewing of a scene enacted on the stage of a fancied theatre of the mind. The idea of seeing-as just invoked brings with it the 'as' intrinsic to imagining. But imagining is not necessarily imaging conceived as the projection of a mental picture. The mentality of imagination is adverbial. How things seem and their seeming as-if are modalities of creative poetic imagining.

Imagining is something we may do. Its being, as Hopkins would say, is a being-doing, a double doing. But not to the exclusion of a certain passivity. This passivity, however, may not be so passive that it excludes the doing inherent to receptivity or the experimentality that sharpens the blade of experience. Philosophers are not altogether misguided when they speak of mental *acts* and include under that term the undergoing of sensory experience and the suffering of feelings or passions. Suffering is twofoldly passion-action. It may be an operation of the will. *Souffrir*, suffering, can be an *ouvrir*, an overture and undergoing in which passivity and activity co-operate. It may be a saying Yes to what fate brings, such affirmation as in the philosophical theology of Scotus and in the poetic theology of Hopkins wills what is willed by a deity. 'Thy will be done.' 'Thy will be-done.' As Hopkins' ultimate categorical imperative could be expressed, 'Let the Creator and his creation be praised.'

Baker's praises of creation are not thus theologically grounded. That is one reason why at this stage of our exposition we are taking our citations from him, not from Hopkins. Baker, unlike Hopkins with his upper-cased notion of Creation, holds by a lower-cased and theology-neutral notion of creation. Yet his celebrations of the natural world are often couched in the language of a general non-institutionalised religiousness.

That is another reason, a more positive one, why in this chapter we are drawing upon the observations made by Baker, rather than Hopkins. Not only are the observations made by Baker not committed to the theistic presuppositions of Hopkins or, as far as I can see, to atheistic or narrowly secular presuppositions; the observations he records in an attitude of scientific representation (and remember that Scotus' observations and arguments are made in defence of *scientia*) are enhanced by representation represented as aesthetico-ethical and broadly politico-religious (and remember that the *scientia* Scotus defends is practical). It is in this second sense that representation can be poetic celebration or song of praise – a sense which, without being of necessity agnosticism, breaks with the presumed antithetical opposition between theistic religion and the religion that preaches with Richard Dawkins at least on some days of the week the gospel of the Absolute Seeming and delusoriness of God.[10]

Baker's 'likenings' and 'seemings' are sometimes so inventively imagined by him that they challenge his reader's powers of imagination, as when, for example,[11] referring to a flock of black-headed gulls, he tells us:

> They too seemed almost transparent in the light of the low-sinking sun. It was an ethereal light, a glowing, holy illumination, hallowing the slender bones, and air threaded marrow of the flaying creature, the lightest, freest, most creative of created things.[12]

Is he, you may ask, talking about a black-headed gull or is he talking about a holy white dove? He could be talking about the former by way of the latter, seeing it as itself, but in so doing bringing his readers to the edge of the world as apocalyptically as does the Avicenno-Scotist horseness of this horse or Géricault's icon of the Prancing Grey Horse in the Burrell Collection in Glasgow.

Baker writes:

> The head of a shire horse comes forward from the fog. It stares in from the mist of the past. Its breath is a starry vapour. The blaze upon its forehead has a supernal shine. The horse seems to be waiting still, after a lifetime of waiting, as though it were watching the inexorable approach of something far-off. Whether it hopes for release, or fears some further bondage, the great eyes cannot reveal. I move nearer, and the head vanishes.[13]

It vanishes as suddenly as the roe deer that

> has come out into the cooler air of the clearing. It is a sudden glow of colour, a rich chestnut-red, like a long legged fox. Its nose twitches, and its big ears move nervously. It is the size of a large dog, very tremulous and slender, with docile, wondering eyes. This is a different place. The deer looks up at the dead beech, listening for familiar sounds. It watches me for half a minute; then it turns, and trots back towards the trees. It stops, and looks round. Then it gallops, leaping like a lamb, bounding away into the beech wood. It has been to the edge of the world.[14]

For the shire horse and the roe deer, but also for Baker, the edge of the world is a quite specific place or unplace, a No Man's Land (possibly a No God's Land) in and out of time. At the beginning of *The Peregrine* he confesses:

> I have always longed to be a part of the outward life. To be out there at the edge of things, to let the human taint wash away in emptiness and silence as the fox sloughs his smell into the cold unworldliness of water; to return to the town as a stranger.[15]

To lose what Hopkins would describe as his self-taste? To be part of what Hopkins would call the world without? At any rate a part of it, not parted from it.

Baker says of a ritual performed between woodpeckers that he observed it 'on an April Sunday lunch-time . . . on the very edge of the world I see, very near to the world beyond the looking-glass, the lost place, the beginning of things'.[16]

Combining physical optics with the metaphysical phenomenology or phenomenography of unfocused slantings or 'sidings' such as we have referred to in speaking of Hopkins, Baker notes:

> Beyond the haze of masts there are bungalows half-hidden by dark Monterey cypresses and wind-lashed Lombardy poplars. The binoculars create a place that does not exist. If I were as close as they pretend, all would look different. Only from here, in the silent privacy of distance and the illusion of the magnifying prisms, is there a wooded land beyond the summer village, a dark mysterious unattainable place, a forest of elms and cypresses and firs.[17]

Hesitating on the threshold of mystery, only the language of seeming seems apt, the language of revelations or Revelations when one cannot believe one's eyes or one's ears, as when

> Many skylarks sing. But in the brief pauses between their songs, the unbroken silence seems to move around me with an immense and primitive power. This is the moor, the rejected land of granite, the green desert of the plutonic rock.[18]

Or as when, still elementally,

> The air had a peculiar density. It was perfectly clear, and the blue sky shone above, yet there seemed to be a silent downward pressure of invisible branches. The air was inhabited, heavy with an unseen presence.[19]

Deprived of its seemings, its impressions, its imaginings and its inscapes, the world lends itself to being seen as the totality of facts that it is said to be in James Gleick's *The Information*.[20] But there is at least one fact to which this pan-informationism turns a blind eye: the fact of its own reflexive seeing-as. Not to mention the unfactual manifold of seemings that spill over the brim of Gleick's literalism, seemings such as those described by Baker and Hopkins. These fall short of or exceed informatic beingness. Their being is a being-doing, the veritative being of the poem of Parmenides of which the being true is the being true of the makar, where the truth is made, performed and produced (*poeiō*), that is to say preceded by a creative act that is not a fact or piece of information, but what Hopkins calls instress and pitch, wondering whether it is identical with what Scotus calls *(h)aecceitas*.

One moral of this chapter is that a distinction must be made between an epistemic distinction that turns on an if-then, and a poetic distinction that turns on an as-if invoked usually for its own sake, though it may sometimes be exercised in the hope that it will serve to promote an increase of scientific knowledge. The observations Hopkins makes in his poems and journals and diaries are made more often than not for the sake of the observations themselves. He would say that they are also made for the greater glory of God, *ad maiorem Dei gloriam*. He could say that they are made to be sung or, like the verb at the heart of the noun of which Carol Ann Duffy writes: danced.

The observations made by Baker too are usually made in language whose literary qualities would capture and hold any reader's attention. Generally, however, Baker's findings do aim to respond to his and our scientific curiosity and add to the sum of, say, ornithological knowledge. As well as delight they produce light. There would seem to be no evidence of a wish on Baker's part, however, to describe that light as supernatural. The nearest he gets to doing that is in his use of the adjective 'supernal'. That does indeed mean celestial, appertaining to the sky, the element in which the falcon peregrinates. But the light of the bird's and of Baker's sky is a natural light, and the watcher's observations belong to natural science. The observations made by Hopkins are observances made within the parameters of a particular organised religion. Not so, it seems to me, the observations made by Baker. This does not mean, however, that they lack a sense of the religious. It does not mean, supposing the language in which they are recorded is, as Wittgenstein might say, 'sublimed' and gone on holiday, that the holiday isn't a holy day, one, among others, along with weekdays, calling to be 'observed'. To show this through Baker's own words was one reason for writing this chapter, to show how much of what we prize in the poetry of Hopkins can survive in such prose as Baker's and hence, in both cases, without depending on theological enlightenment; so without supposing that 'Cross' is a good gloss for the word 'Crux' as used in the title of my first chapter to identify the primary reason for writing this book as stated in that first chapter's last paragraph.

8
Peirce's Post-Kantian Categories

The attainment of scientific enlightenment is the chief end for which Charles Sanders Peirce constructs the theorems, theories and systems whose logical structures are described in his writings. Could we sum up the differences and similarities at issue here between him, Hopkins and Baker by saying that whereas in the poetic works of Hopkins, including among them parts of his journals, the as-if is dominant but capable of subserving the if-then of science, and that whereas in Baker's journals the as-if and the if-then are of roughly equal importance, in the structures Peirce describes and constructs, the if-then is more profoundly engaged than the as-if? Almost, but not without oversimplification. To adopt this perspective would be to pay too little heed to the temporal and logical priorities of scientific research and to the place in it occupied by what Peirce calls abduction or retroduction, meaning by that the formation of hypotheses. Abduction is retroduction because it looks back to observations that have already been made, such observations as some of those made by Baker and Hopkins. But it also looks forward to observations that have not yet been made. A hypothesis is a prediction of a law or model proposed by the imagination prompted by observations made so far, and by guesses with regard to what future experience or experiment may bring. As an educated guess at how the facts will bear out or fail to bear out the imagined hypothesis the connective if-then will also be brought into action. This action is the making of the step from the as-if – Hopkins' pattern or design – to the if-then. It is the step that determines whether a currently held hypothesis will be maintained.

This 'will be' is a large part of what Peirce wishes to highlight in what he understands by 'pragmatism', later 'pragmaticism', defined as the view that 'there is no distinction of meaning so fine as to consist in anything but a possible difference of practice'.[1] Peirce continues the tradition to which Scotus and Hopkins belong of putting emphasis upon the fundamentality of praxis. By practice, Peirce means habit and by habit he means a disposition in which someone or something would behave in such and such an in principle observable way if such and such conditions obtained. I say 'someone or something' because the so-called habit may be that of a living being or of something inorganic. As with Hopkins, a power may be had (*habitus*) either by a self that can say of itself and of 'the world within' 'I find myself . . .', or by something in 'the world without'.[2] Or by both together in so far as every passive power corresponds to an active power, as implied by Locke when he writes: 'Thus we say, Fire has a power to melt gold, i.e. to destroy the consistency of its insensible parts, and consequently its hardness, and make it fluid; and gold has a power to be melted; that the sun has a power to blanch wax, and wax a power to be blanched by the sun, whereby the yellowness is destroyed, and whiteness made to exist in its room.'[3] This is the behabitive relationality Locke intends when he writes two sections later that 'power includes relation'.

On this Peirce agrees with Locke. He agrees with him too that this relation is predominantly a relation with the future. He would, however, question Locke's statement in the same section that 'Our idea therefore of power . . . may well have a place amongst other simple ideas, and be considered as one of them; being one of those that make a principal ingredient in our complex ideas of substances, as we shall hereafter have occasion to observe.' What we thereafter have occasion to observe is that substance is, among other things, solidity. By this Locke could be meaning a primary quality belonging to the realm of the corpuscular bodies that according to him, following Boyle, occasion our ideas of secondary qualities.[4] On the other hand he could be meaning the secondary quality of felt resistance to which the solidity of the underlying substance gives rise when a diamond for example is pressed.[5]

Taken in this second sense what Locke calls the simple secondary quality would be what Peirce too calls a quality, one falling under his category of Firstness. However, Peirce also refers to Firstness as 'pure may-be' and 'positive qualitative possibility'.[6] That is to say, where Locke appears to be in danger of reducing the relationality of the idea of solidity to a simple, Peirce courts the risk of confusing the Firstness of quality with the Thirdness of the conditionality, potentiality or, here, possibility. Perhaps that risk is one he welcomes. For it is an implication of the futural orientation of pragmatism as he understands it. But if he is to embrace this risk he must do so without embracing self-contradiction. He could do this by embracing dialectic, as the numerical names for his categories indicate that he does. Doing that would enable him to hold that although a quality like redness can count as a case of Firstness on the grounds that it is, to use Locke's word, simple by comparison with cases of Thirdness and Secondness (explained below), what it is for something to be red can be explained in practice only via and through (*dia*) these more explicitly relational and operational categories. The most explicitly relational and operational of these is Thirdness, where the explicitness is that of the if-then, notwithstanding that some of the possibilities thus spelled out will be counterfactual. These possibilities could be described as impure and complex in order to distinguish them from the 'pure qualitative' possibilities of Firstness. The latter are pure, each a 'pure may-be', in that the quality in question, for instance a redness, does not act on and is not acted upon by something else. The redness may not in fact be exemplified and may never have been exemplified by anything in the universe – not even the redness of the blood of which Hopkins writes in his pages on Parmenides or possibly the blood of Christ. The redness may be a not yet applied quality, the quality of nothing, something like the fresh colour of the freshly squeezed unused pigment on a painter's palate or rather – since the colour of the pigment already 'inheres' in the pigment and in the palate on to which it is squeezed – like a Platonic Idea of, say, Redness, or like the redness of Christ's blood before it was shed, or, to use Peirce's own words, like 'What the world was to Adam on the day he opened his eyes to it, before he had drawn any distinctions, or become conscious of his own existence – that is first, present, immediate, fresh, new, initiative, original, spontaneous, free, vivid, conscious, and evanescent', or, to use Hopkins' word again, 'flush', or, to borrow from Kant, 'less even than a dream', even the dream that Adam had (*Critique of Pure Reason*, A 112). But the possibility of the redness being actualised has always already been positively real. 'Only, remember that every description of it must be false to it' and that 'we can know nothing of such possibilities [except] so far as they are actualised'.[7]

In Peirce's terminology to be actualised means to exist, where existence is intermediate between the purely qualitative presence of Firstness and the lawfulness of Thirdness in the triad of categories of being based on Kant's list which he substitutes for the traditional Aristotelo-Scholastic decad. This substitution goes along with an endorsement of Scholasticism in that the affirmation by some Schoolmen of the reality of universals is succeeded by Peirce's arguments for the metaphysical reality of power and law. So he is able to call himself a Scholastic realist, a subscriber to the philosophical analysis to which nominalism objects when it denies that there is any generality other than the sameness or synonymy of names. No term of abuse is more common in Peirce's lexicon than 'Nominalism', a malediction he levels not only against medieval nominalists like Ockham but also against Descartes, Hobbes, the 'British Empiricists' and Locke. This is what makes Peirce so instructive a guide to the misunderstandings of which medieval thinkers and philosophers of science have been rightly or wrongly accused. Despite his relentless criticism of nominalism he shares its distaste for substantial forms or natural kinds regarded as entities. He holds that the debate between realists and nominalists rests on a failure, paradoxically one encouraged by the uncritical talk of entities on the part of the Scotists, to recognise that a non-entitive way of speaking of natural kinds is feasible, as Peirce will himself attempt to demonstrate with his analysis in terms of the 'would-be' and 'would-do' of Thirdness. As for the moderns, 'when the new men denied that the substantial forms were "entities", what they really had in mind was that those forms had not such a mode of being as would confer upon them the power dynamical to react upon other things'.[8] This 'power dynamical' would be the power, for example, of the invisible corpuscular substances which, according to Locke, cause our ideas of a visible object's primary qualities. Note that here physically causal explanation has taken over from the metaphysical explanations of the old school except that, according to Peirce, the metaphysics of 'something I know not what' or 'the thing in itself' survives. These, he holds, are corollaries of nominalism which are insufficiently complex to meet the demands of Peirce's relationalist realism of possibility and legal necessity. They therefore lack the complexity of the theory of signs which he appends to his theory of categories rather as Locke's *Essay* passes to a book discussing words from two books discussing ideas, and as a theory of signification and meaning is appended to a theory of categories in the treatise Heidegger attributes to Scotus.

In connection with this transition from theory of categories to hermeneutic of signs, a closer analogy between Heidegger and Peirce merits mention. Heidegger, it will be recalled, maintains that interpretation is ultimately circular. He also maintains that circularity is not vicious provided we take care to enter the circle at the right place. Peirce holds that thoughts are signs, that signs have significations that are in turn signs for an interpretant, and therefore that thinking is in principle circular. Is it also infinitely regressive or infinitely progressive? Does it effect an asymptotic convergence or does it posit the attainment of a goal? It could do both if the goal were the aquisition of a habit.

Pragmatism or pragmaticism is practicalism. And it does not matter for practical purposes if the exercise of the habit in question occasionally leads to observations that are unexpected. That is the way knowledge grows. But, it may be asked, what about the chances of reaching knowledge as to whether the growth of knowledge might come to an end with, say, the coming of the end of the world? If Peirce is to answer this question about knowledge he must first answer a question about meaning. He states that it is possible to reach 'the entire general intended interpretant', the 'very meaning', an 'adequate ultimate interpretation'. How can this statement be reconciled with his statement that the interpretant of a sign can be 'in turn a sign, and so on *ad infinitum*' (his emphasis)?[9] At least one step towards an answer to this last question is made once counterfactual conditionality is given room in the conditionality that is, we have discovered, the key to an understanding of Peirce's realist (one might say social-realist) account of meaning. That account is framed in terms of the notion of an infinite regress or progress of representative signs interpreted by representative signs interpreted by . . ., and so on. But the series has to be distinguished from the meaning conveyed by a sign. The meaning is not the finite or infinite series. It is a habit or practice conveyed by the series, and that in turn is not the sort of thing of which it makes sense to ask whether it is finite or infinite.[10]

With its emphasis on law and intersubjectivity, this characterisation of the category of Thirdness sounds not a little Hegelian. That is how it sounds to John Boler.[11] He cites Peirce's statement that 'pragmatism is closely allied to the Hegelian absolute idealism . . .' But Peirce goes on immediately to describe this idealism as that 'from which . . . it [pragmatism] is sundered by its vigorous denial that the third category (which Hegel degrades to a mere stage of thinking) suffices to make the world, or is even so much as self-sufficient'.[12] Elsewhere he announces, 'My whole method will be found to be in contrast with that of Hegel; I reject his philosophy *in toto.*'[13] He rejects it, he explains, because Hegel forgets the categories of Firstness and Secondness.

Firstness is 'the mode of being which consists in its subject's being positively such as it is regardless of aught else', for instance the mode of being a redness, where the only connection with something else would be likeness, the sphere we have explored with the help of J. A. Baker's graphic descriptions of sightings of the natural world, Hopkins' inscapes and what Scotus calls common natures.

Secondness is 'a mode of being of one thing which consists in how a second subject is', the fact 'that there is a real world with actions and reactions', actuality, existence. There is more than a hint here of the notion that existence denotes something that arises from something (ex), from what we conceive as the cause of a thing or of an event enacted or effected (e, ex) or caused. Hopkins the philologist and etymologist would tell us that Latin *causa* becomes French *chose*, thing, some thing that may remain unrevealed, at most glimpsed, like the elusive aspect of an inscape, the partially hidden history to which it looks back. The duality implied in secondness here is that of cause and effect or explanation and what is explained. But the phrases just cited from Peirce here in this causal context will remind the vigilant reader of those remarkable ones concerning 'sakes' and *Sache* cited early in our second chapter from a letter Hopkins sent Bridges. So remarkable are those already cited phrases that part of the paragraph in which they occur merits reproduction here in order to facilitate comparison. Referring to the word 'sake', and separating with an 'and also' levels from meta-levels of quiddity, Hopkins tells Bridges,

> I mean by it the being a thing has outside of itself, as a voice by its echo, a face by its reflection, a body by its shadow, a man by his name, fame, or memory, *and also* that in the thing by virtue of which especially it has this being abroad, and that is something distinctive, marked, specifically or individually speaking, as for a voice and echo clearness; for a reflected image light, brightness; for a shadow-casting body bulk; for a man genius, great achievements, amiability, and so on.[14]

When we read Peirce's statement that Secondness is 'a mode of being of one thing which consists in how a second subject is' it is difficult to avoid thinking of Hopkins' reference to 'the being a thing has outside itself'. Peirce, we have agreed, has in mind causal relationships, and in the light of what he says about the structure of Thirdness in terms of which Secondness has ultimately to be fleshed out we must construe causal relationships as instantiations of the form if-then. But the generality or (because being is not a genus) 'generality' of the two similar phrases used by Peirce and Hopkins allows the possibility of their being construed according to the form as-if. This is the form of seeming and representation in terms of which we distinguished Hopkins' and certain of Baker's poietically creative sentences from the scientific prose of the natural world that those rapt sentences of Baker's were, it seems to me, intended by him to subserve. It is the form of representation in which we said Cézanne is engaged when in his studies of the Mont Sainte Victoire he was representing the mountain not by way of simple reproduction but out of love for it, for the mountain's own unreproducible sake, in the same way that in Hopkins' celebration of the inscapes of the world representation is not just imitative but, to use our barbarous word, aesthethical.

We have by no means exhausted the goldmine of the explanation Hopkins offered to Bridges of what he meant by 'sake' and by a thing's 'being abroad'. We shall return in later chapters to further explore the ramifications of these rich veins. Right now we return to Charles Sanders Peirce.

Peirce tells us that his own list of categories grew out of a study of Kant's. Kant himself, 'the King of modern thought',[15] remarks in the *Critique of Pure Reason* that his table of categories 'suggests some nice points' (B 109). Among these nice points may be counted the fact that existence and non-existence and the other members of his triad of modalities apply via the other three triads. This is already a good reason for holding that existence is not a first level predicate. That Peirce holds this is exhibited by his distinction of Secondness from Firstness and Thirdness. Yet his efforts at explaining what we and he himself understand by existence are so clad in metaphor that they could be taken as evidence that existence is richly predicative. I shall ignore his tropes of pushing against doors and of feeling the constable's hand on one's shoulder. I take my lead instead from his granting that there is what he deems to be a degenerate sense of existence that is based on bare reference. Degenerate though it may be, it is the sense Heidegger tells us was fundamental in medieval and classical discourse, that of simple ontic presence at hand. I take my lead from that sense of existence because it is to the ontic, to beings, that I want to restore any recognition and dignity that they may seem to have been denied by attempts such as Heidegger's to do justice to being. I take my lead here from Peirce's unadorned version of 'individual' and his degenerate version of 'existence' in the hope that they will take me back to Duns Scotus, to Hopkins' reading of *haecceitas*, and to the 'be' of beings. I do this in full awareness of the paradoxicality of my procedure. This paradoxicality consists in the ravelledness of explaining with explaining away. Right from the first words about Hopkins in this book I appear to have been solemnly engaged in defeating what I take to be this poet's purpose, namely, by neologisms, for instance 'inscape' and 'instress', to return strangeness to terms that have lost their savour, for instance the terms 'essence' and 'existence'. The latter, 'existence', is the one that we have now found Peirce attempting to wake from its dogmatic slumber. Then I come along and spoil it all by trying to explain what the Jesuit poet and the Franciscan logician may mean, attempting to do that by translating their coinages and remintings back into the ready cash of current currency. I explain, it seems, by explaining away. This is one reason why at a late stage of this book I temporarily abandoned commentary on Hopkins and Scotus in favour of commentary on citations from Baker. This was a shift of attention from the language of poetry to the language, still often sublimely poetic, of an author whose purposes are sublimely scientific. Were it not for the visionary depth that turns Baker's observations into quasi-liturgical religious observance, reading him would be like reading 'The Philosopher', whether by this emphatically definite description is meant Aristotle or, to ring the changes, Duns Scotus. Were it not for the singing tones in which Baker, like Lucretius in his poem *De rerum natura*, delivers his natural scientific findings, one could imagine while reading him that one was reading instead the pages on which Aristotle accumulates his findings, or the pages on which information about such accumulation is filed under the word 'induction' in the collected papers of Peirce.

The word 'like' occurs in the last paragraph. The word 'likeness' occurs passim throughout the pages by which that paragraph is preceded. One of the reasons for this is that, as mentioned there, the 'x is like y' form of comparison is more at home in the field of scientific observation than it is in poetry, notwithstanding the bardic setting of 'My love is like a red, red rose.' And if anybody asks you 'Shall I compare thee to a summer's day?' answer No. Comparisons are invidious. Ask instead for a metaphor. For metaphor is at once more intimate and more respectful than simile is of your identity and of your individuality, a certain Scotist conception of individuality being the theme that runs through the entire length of this study parallel with the axis connecting and separating intention and attention. Hence formulae incorporating the prepositional 'like' are rare throughout the poetic writings of Hopkins in comparison with the rather more scientifically objective writings of Baker. This is why we turned to the latter in order to begin to get a feel for the difference between the kind of analogy typical of poetry, represented by Hopkins, and the kind of analogy typical of science, represented in the subject matter of Peirce's philosophy of science, the 'between' of this philosophico-logical comparison being represented by the mixed rhetorics of Baker. This triad shows that it is possible to be not only *between* two minds but *in* two minds. This possibility in turn shows that although the paradox of explanation mentioned above presents a difficulty, it is a difficulty that, with exercise of the imagination, may be circumvented, especially if we acknowledge the possibility of being in two minds by respelling imagination as imadgination. This is a 'barbarism' coined by me precisely to keep open room for barbarisms like Hopkins' 'being-do', which we know he himself describes as a barbarism. He could have said the same about 'inscape' and 'instress', neologisms we tried to explain, paradoxically, in terms of the very paleologisms, for instance 'essence' and 'existence', which the new words were meant to reinvigorate or replace.

Likewise with 'imadgination'. It is touched by the lunacy that Hopkins refers to as strangeness or queerness and that we have referred to as quaintance. It is 'mad' in so far as it is in two minds, schizzoid. The two minds are reflected in the distinction between intellectual powers and active powers made in titles of two essays by that other Scottish philosopher Thomas Reid to whom Peirce refers as 'that singularly accurate observer' and, aware that he is borrowing an adjective used widely of Scotus, 'that subtle but well-balanced intellect'. Would we be attributing a degree of unbalance to that intellect if we said that the term of art 'imadgination' (and imadgination is indeed an art) could well have figured in the title of a third work, intermediate between those two essays by Reid, a work for which the raw materials are made available by Kant, another of Peirce's heroes – and arguably, with his name spelled as Cant, another Scot?[16] If we would, observe too that we would be attributing thereby also a compensating degree of balance. For that third work would mediate between *theōria* and *praxis*, like the visible or invisible hyphen in Hopkins' conception of being as also doing, so as mind translated both as intellect and mind translated as minding, being mindful, what Scotus calls will as an expression of love, which we shall later spell out as will not to will.

In 1868, four years before Hopkins fell in love with Scotus, Peirce wrote:

> The great argument for nominalism is that there is no man unless there is some particular man. That, however, does not affect the realism of Scotus; for although there is no man of whom all further determination can be denied, yet there is a man, abstraction made of all further determination. There is a real difference between man irrespective of what the other determinations may be, and man with this or that particular series of determinations, although undoubtedly this difference may be relative to the mind and not *in re*. Such is the position of Scotus.[17]

In support of this last sentence Peirce cites from Scotus himself: *Eadem natura est, quae in existentia, per gradum singularitatis est determinata, et in intellectu, hoc est ut habet relationem ad intellectum ut cognitum ad cognoscens, est indeterminata.*[18] That is to say, placed in context:

> Therefore the universal can be in the things in such a way that it is the same nature which in the existential order is determined by a particular grade of singularity and is in the intellect; that is to say, as having a relationship to the intellect as what is known to the knower it is indeterminate.[19]

The relativity to mind mentioned here is that of the varying determinations in spite of which the reality of the generality of manhood is sustained. The point is made succinctly a few paragraphs earlier:

> The nominalists, I suspect, confound together thinking a triangle without thinking that it is either equilateral, isosceles, or scalene, and thinking a triangle without thinking whether it is equilateral, isosceles, or scalene.[20]

The word 'existence' is notable by its absence from this geometrical illustration. It would not necessarily be omitted from that mathematical universe of discourse by Scotus (or by modern theorists of mathematics). Nor, where it is used by Scotus in non-mathematical fields such as that of humanity referred to in the earlier citation from Pcirce, would the word 'existence' enter on the scene with the shock and brute force Peirce attributes to it. We have seen that, in Scotus' references to existence, existence or being (*esse*) can be said of essence (*essentia*). Vis-à-vis Scotus, Peirce is changing the subject and talking at cross purposes with him. This is confirmed if we recall that the root of existence expressed in *ek-sisto* conveys the notion of historical coming-from, as do the forms *esse* and *essentia* (and as does the Welsh for 'essence', namely *hanfod*, where *han* is cognate with *hanes*, history). The essence of something is that from which it originates. It alludes to a ground or cause. If such an allusion is made by *ex-sisto* as cited by Peirce as a clue to what he understands by existence, the cause is a final cause bridging the gap between potentiality and the corresponding realisation of this as entelechy. 'Whatever exists, *ex-sists*, that is, really acts upon other existents, so obtains a self-identity, and is definitely individual.'[21] It belongs to 'the mode of being . . . of an individual thing or fact, the being which consists in the object's crowding out a place for itself in the universe, so to speak, and reacting by brute force of fact, against all other things. I shall call that existence'.[22]

Calling is something we do with signs. Acknowledgement of this draws our attention to the fact that, whatever one's view about who was the author of the second part of the *Theory of Categories and Signification*, none would doubt that Peirce is the author of an elaborate theory of signs. Without investigating here the minutiae of that theory, we cannot but be struck by the parallelism of the relation between the distinctions made in that theory and the distinctions made in what he challengingly names his 'phenomenology', meaning by that his theory of categories, and meaning by so naming it to throw down the gauntlet to, among others, Hegel. We know that Peirce criticises Hegel for not sufficiently stressing the category of Secondness. If we accept that Peirce's theory of signs is in parallel with his theory of categories, his criticism of Hegel's alleged failure to do justice to the role of Secondness and therefore of existence and individuality will be reflected in what he would think of the attitude he would expect Hegel to adopt with regard to the 'index'. The index is the second kind of sign in Peirce's list, between the icon and the symbol, assuming that these correspond respectively to the categories of pure quality and lawful and law-full disposition. On the one hand, then, Pierce shies away from Hegel's niggardly treatment of indication mocked in the *Phenomenology of Mind* under the heading of sense certainty (compare Derrida's 'deconstruction' of what he regards as the niggardly treatment of indication meted out in the phenomenology of Husserl). On the other hand, Peirce scolds Locke and the British Empiricists for being too generous to indication.

Indication is pointing, pointing for instance to what we point to by pointing and saying 'this' or 'that'. This must have its place in any theory of significative meaning and intending. And Peirce is consistent when, following the clue of a forwardly oriented analysis of the category of *ex-sisto*, he confers upon himself in his theory of signification the right to interpret indication, the signative partner of the category of existence, as pointing ahead. If we follow him in doing this, however, let us take care not to miss the trick Hopkins brings off in his reading of Scotus. To miss that would be to miss the opportunity to understand how the instress of doing implicit in being allows us to glimpse an inscape of how pointing-to and intentionality look back and forward to attentionality, that is to say to looking, and to being pointed at. We shall take that opportunity in the next chapter. In that chapter too we shall take the opportunity to defend Hopkins against the charge of a confusion we must mention before ending this chapter on Peirce, for we think that the charge is one against which Peirce cannot be defended.

Peirce carries out a 'denigration' of individuality as he takes Scotus to understand individuality.[23] He accuses him of being a closet nominalist. He is that, Peirce holds, partly because he excludes from Secondness, so from the individual existent, the laws and would-be's of Thirdness. Such is his charge against Scotus. But would not Scotus reply that this charge turns a blind eye to the logic or metaphysics of formal distinction according to which the terms distinguished are really inseparable? In Scotus' language the terms are individuality on the one hand and metaphysical common nature on the other. There is a 'confusion', but it is not one that exists only in Peirce's thinking. It is one that exists in individual objective reality. His attempt at a denigration of individuality confuses what is individual with the haecceity that, in combination with the nature, makes the individual possible, actual and existent.[24] Despite this, I welcome the emphasis that, in his criticism of Hegel, he puts on existence. For, as I remind the reader of this book from time to time, I take existence to be a route via goodness to an increase in scope of responsibility and of regard in both the optical and the ethical – the aesthethical – senses of this word.

9

Ecceity, Ipseity and Existents

I find myself hoping that one small step for non-humankind as well as humankind might be made by daring to think that Heidegger's categories of the world-constructing (*weltbildend*), the poor in world (*weltarm*) and the worldless (*weltlos*) can be transcended to what the Scholastics referred to as Transcendentals, namely Being, Unity, the True, the Good (and possibly the Beautiful). If these are most common notions that hold of being they would seem to hold of being when this is understood as existence in abstraction from properties and predicates. But the traditional doctrine maintains that the transcendentals are coextensive with one another. As regards being as sheer existence, its overlap with the Good is displayed in what I make bold to describe as the fact that a thing's existence is a good to that thing. But this 'fact' has something like the status of what Kant has in mind when he refers to the moral law as a *Faktum* of reason. His moral law, also what Plato refers to sometimes as the Good and sometimes as the Idea of the Good, and Levinas' notion of the good as ethicality are, I argue, implicated and somehow complicit with existence or being in what Levinas refers to as an intrigue. This intrication won't answer the limitrophic questions we have to face from time to time, questions of where and when to draw the line. But it can teach us that otherness is the only 'category' that operates in the thought that the pure existence of something other than ourselves imposes on us a responsibility that is logically prior to predication.

Also logically prior to predication is address. Address and existence are partners in something like what Scotus dubs *distinctio formalis*. The distinctness of the terms in a formal distinction goes along with their real as distinct from solely logical inseparability. Paradigm cases of this for Scotus and his contemporaries are the relations between God and His attributes, the relation of the Persons of the Trinity and the relation between the will and the intellect in the human person. But address breaks up formality in the way that prescription suspends description, that something assertively said is disrupted by the speech-action of possibly non-assertive saying, and in the way that constatement and performance are inextricable from each other. So, not being a relation between terms, the chiasmus of address and existence would be more accurately labeled a *distinctio deformalis* or a *distinctio quasi-formalis* or a *distinctio formalis deformata*. Address is the appeal that the sheer existence of something or someone makes in which the goodness for that entity of its existence attracts our attention. The appeal is the call (*appel*, *Geheiss*, vocation) 'Listen!' or 'Look!' It is the '*Ecce*' that can be heard or seen in the haecceity of the individuated singularity that according to Scotus, followed by Hopkins, is in a relation of formal distinction with a thing's common nature. In Scotus' usual account stress is put on the individuated entity in its capacity of being pointed at. Pointing is accomplished from a point, the pointer's point of view, the origin of the scope and of the scape she or he surveys within which entities are observed and from which some look at or look to the observer. The movement of the gesture is outward, centrifugal, 'ec-static' in the sense of the word given it by Heidegger, who came to the composition of *Being and Time* well versed in Scotism, having written a dissertation on it. So if Levinas' thinking can be considered a 'reversal' of Heidegger's in *Being and Time* and via that inspired at least unconsciously by Scotus' stress on singularity, we shall expect that that stress will be carried not primarily by pointing, *deixis*, but primarily by address directed at an addressee who refers to him- or herself as 'me' or 'myself', as in Hopkins' 'I find myself . . .'

Although Scotus sometimes appears to teach the opposite,[1] he maintains that existence is really the same as essence, '*esse* est idem realiter cum *essentia*'.[2] This is a doctrine that makes it easier to understand how, against Aquinas, Scotus can endorse Anselm's argument for the necessity of the existence of God provided it incorporates a clause specifying that the concept of the highest thinkable being is free from contradiction.[3] But while the assertion that existence is really the same as essence may be acceptable in the strictly theological context where existence is one of God's perfections, it is not obviously in order where created real things are concerned. True, in the context of these last we could still maintain a distinction between existence and essence by distinguishing first order predicates or their metaphysical equivalents from second order predicates or their metaphysical equivalents, regarding existence as a second order predicate and what Scotus would apparently not allow us to separate from essence. But such multiplication of levels of predicativity would be a curious way by which to attempt to establish on an appeal to non-predicativity a hope of making what the opening sentence of this chapter refers to as one small step for non-humankind and humankind.[4]

A different distinction of orders or levels is made by Scotus' compatriot David Hume when the latter writes: 'The idea of existence, then, is the very same with the idea of what we conceive to be existent' and 'Whatever we conceive, we conceive to be existent.'[5] This could be taken to identify existence and idea or conception or essence, as though, more ambitious than Anselm, Hume is saying that to conceive a thing is to conceive that it exists understood as judging that it exists, whereas what he is saying is that to conceive a thing is to conceive it *as* existing, as a *possible* existent, despite the difficulty entailed by the temptation to construe the idea of possibility as an impression.

Whether or not this is accepted as a correct reading of Hume, once we make the distinction between separation and distinction as made by Scotus we may see a way around the threat that the latter's view of the relation of existence to essence may seem to hold for our attempt to recruit him to our cause. His sentence 'Existence is really the same as essence' does not deny a conceptual distinction. It does not even deny a conceptual distinction on conceptual grounds. It denies a separability in reality, *realiter* or *a parte rei*. It affirms a *distinctio formalis*. So he can even reify what we have just called a possible existent as a possibility or an essence that exists, though at a higher level of existence, the level of second or higher intentionality. Given this hierarchy, even an essence can be an existent and an existent in which existence is metaphysically and not only logically univocal. Moreover, its existence would suffice to serve as a basis for speaking of the goodness for that existent of its existence, unless we are persuaded by nominalists such as William of Ockham that instead of stressing the 'moreover' just mentioned we should stress the 'much-less' that results from refusing to admit the existence of more entities than are necessary. But necessary for what? Necessary, Scotus maintains, for safeguarding the possibility of science, whether metaphysical or physical or, with widely acknowledged limitations that recognise the difference between faith and reason, theological. *Scientia*, Scotus maintains, requires the real existence of essences. The Hopkins of the essay on Parmenides would agree. His interpretation of Parmenides is tantamount to a demonstation that without real essences we would be left without the possibility of 'stress'. We would be left at most with the possibility of thinking of thinking and of saying as the appending of proper names. Now the latter seems to be the conception Hopkins entertains at least sometimes when from the philosophical universe of discourse he moves to that of poetry. Pierre (Derrida) Alféri writes:

Gerard Manley Hopkins thought of poetry precisely as a twist inflicted upon language in order to assimilate it to the use of proper names or to an idiom that is absolutely faithful to the thing's signature, to the sensible-intelligible essence of it which he called the *inscape*. In doing this he invoked Duns Scotus for support. But Ockham thought the *being-this*, Scotist haecceity, more radically than Scotus himself. This originary *phenomenon* that constitutes the being as this thing, before all subjective elaboration, is the unique object of Ockham's reduced ontology.[6]

The phrase 'sensible-intelligible essence' hints at the notion of a 'unique object' that is common to knowledge of the natural world and to poetry. (In some respects it also anticipates the irreducibly 'originary' ambiguous operation that Kant calls schematism and assigns to imagination.)[7] Resisting the idea that inscape, as formally distinct from instress, *is* haecceity, we have seen reason to regard inscape *as a vehicle of* haecceity. We shall not take up here the question how Ockham might have responded to a reading of Scotus that followed Hopkins in shaving from this word its initial letter 'h' thereby showing that pointing presupposes address. Nor shall we consider here the grounds for and against the validity of the objection sometimes made against Ockham that his argument against the realism of Scotus' conception of formal distinction ultimately begs the question.[8] Instead, we shall turn from the ingenious linkage Derrida *fils* forges between Ockham, Scotus and Hopkins in order to consider briefly instead the interrelation between these and Heidegger that is unravelled in the last seminars of Derrida *père*.

Jacques Derrida refers to Hopkins and, indirectly through the latter, to Scotus in a paper mentioned in editorial footnotes at the beginning and end of the second volume of *The Beast and the Sovereign*.[9] Derrida's invocation of Hopkins is prompted by the poet's powerful prose meditation on the eachness of his and our being towards death that Heidegger calls *Jemeinigkeit* in *Being and Time* and calls *Einsamkeit*, solitude, in *The Fundamental Concepts of Metaphysics*. Our reflections on this question run up against the problem encountered earlier[10] of circumventing the barrier which the second syllable of 'thisness' seems to place in the way of our finding a non-general referent for its first syllable 'this'. The same problem, unless it is a pseudoproblem, has now been posed by 'eachness'. It is posed by *individualitas* and by *haecceitas*, the word Hopkins was so glad to have come across in his reading of Duns Scotus. Hopkins does not exactly solve that problem. What he does is to leave it in Scotus' lap, allowing Scotus to hold, if he wishes, that the relation between a common nature and an individuated singular referent is one of *distinctio formalis*, but bringing to our attention that this relation depends on a quasi-relation hidden in it in the way *ecce* is encapsulated in *haecceitas*. For, having followed faithfully Scotus' spelling *haecceitas*, lo and behold, all at once (*exaiphnēs*) he spells it without the aitch. 'Is not this pitch or whatever we call it then the same as Scotus' ecce*itas*?'[11] Whatever else we call pitch, Hopkins also calls it stress. This in turn gets explained by him in terms of freedom and will, as exercised in the affirming of judgements as to being and beings and in the doing of justice and injustice. However, the word Hopkins reads in or into Scotus' writings still leaves us with *-itas*, the Latin marker for second intentional 'ness', 'nessness', 'nesshood', 'hoodness' and 'hoodhood', though our attention is now turned to *ecce*, meaning 'Attend', in the imperative mood, which is 'performative' in Derrida's widened sense of Austin's technical term. So *ecceitas* itself, which purports to be a partner with common nature combined or, rather, chiasmically crossed in a formal distinction, already incorporates a formal relation between performativity and constativity. It does this in a complex speech act where the form of the formality shatters against and is divided by the individuating and isolating power of address. This isolating is effected by this addressing, for addressing is not a mode of being-with, but a prior call to attention.

Hopkins' unorthodox orthography gains some legitimacy from the fact that an earlier form of *haec* is *haece*, where *ec* is the root of the Latin word *oculus*, eye. His revision turns demonstration into invitation or request or command. Note that *ecce* is also part of the word in its more usual aspirated form, crossing performativity with constatement and hinting at an imperativity implicit in and disnominative of its abstract nominality. This is brought out brilliantly by Derrida for the context of constitutional law in the first part of *Otobiographies*, where the relevant sensory organ is no longer the *oculus*, the *oeil*, but the *otos*, the ear.[12]

Ecce!: '*ecce*' highlights (emphasises, stresses) the appellative function performed by the word 'Note' as addressed to the reader at the beginning of the third sentence in the paragraph directly preceding this one. It says 'mark my word' or 'NB', *nota bene*. If it is referentially intentive, its *intentio* is supported and transported by the attentive and apocalyptive vehicles of such categorical imperatives as 'Look', 'Look here', 'Listen', 'Lo', 'Behold' and 'Lo and behold'.

These imperatives are absolutely categorical in the sense that even in disobeying them we obey them. If we decide not to heed them, not to comply with the request 'Heed' or 'Read' that each of them makes, we have heeded or read them nonetheless. Our doing either is the corollary of our having said Yes to communication of some sort or unsort. And to do that, we gather from Hopkins' comments on Parmenides, is to say a 'simple *yes*' to Being. So if how the principle of individuation works is beset by incommunicability, as Scotus says explicitly and as Hopkins implies that it is, it will be an incommunicability that presupposes the absolute communicability betrayed by the possibility of these and other thinkers asking themselves whether the secret of how individuation works can be communicated. What Scotus declares to be incommunicable is the contraction of the common nature to something that is by definition uncommon, the differentia of the individuable, that is to say of what cannot be shared by this item and that item and thet item and thot. The very function performed in this contraction of the sharable to the unsharable prohibits it from becoming common property. Although one of the terms of this operation is common, its other component is ex hypothesi singular. So only what Scotus calls the common nature can reveal itself within the horizons laid open by the imperative 'Look' and by the looking which is the human addressee's stressed, willed, response. The singularity as such of an individuated entity and of the *causa* of that individuation remain at the threshold between the categorial constatement of the as suchness of the *-itas* of *haecceitas* and the categorically imperative and addressive performativity of the *ecce* of *ecceitas*.

Who within the economy commanded by the imperative *ecce* addresses this imperative 'Look'? To whom is it addressed? To what or to whom is the addresser asking the addressee to address him- or herself? The imperatives 'Look at me' (*ecce me*), 'Look at you' (*ecce te*), 'Look at her' (*ecce eam*), 'Look at this' (*ecce id*), 'Look at us' (*ecce nos*), 'Look at them' (*ecce ea*) jointly construct the spatiality of justices in which 'justices' is understood as either a verb or a plural noun by Derrida and Hillis Miller citing Hopkins' words 'the just man justices' from a poem that will be cited again below. 'Justices' even taken as a plural noun retains the imperativity signified by its Latin root *ius*, meaning command or demand. This meaning calls to be distinguished for the same reason that the plurality of the noun 'justices' calls to be admitted into the lexicon, namely in order to save the difference that is made according to who addresses the imperative and to whom the imperative is addressed. Is the first person singular individual that is called upon to be just in a position to call for others to do justice to him or to her? This is the difference of which we are reminded by Levinas' conception of justice and of an equality that is not entailed by universal justice in that his conception of equality is one where equality can be claimed on my behalf by others but not on my behalf by myself.

Because justice is something done or something that fails to be done it is natural that a verbal form should be made available that expresses its grammar. Furthermore, the noun 'justice' earns the right to be put in the plural as a mark of recognition that where universal justice reigns (*waltet*) there reigns violence (*Gewalt*) even when systematic justice is not deaf to the demand for justice to the individual existent independent of whatever may be the primary predicates that appertain to that individual. Not even the all-embracing justice that is called *dikē* in the language of Sophocles can suspend the reciprocal violence between universal and singular justices. This is because, as described in the language of Scotus, the maximally determinate individuality of the individual is at the same time the maximally indeterminate point of focus towards which common concepts may be contracted. Another reason for this is that the relation between the common nature and the singularity and its ground is one of formal distinction, one in which the terms are distinguished but the things they stand for in reality are not separable. This relation can be understood only if we maintain the distinction we made in Chapter 5 between two kinds of contraction. One kind of contraction is the continuous though possibly unsmooth or stepwise densification and intensification within the zone of the predicable common natures and their modes proceeding either from a genus to a species or within a genus or species towards a thicker or thinner specification. Another kind of contraction is the sudden one from the logical space of predicates and natures or essence to the zone of individuality and sheer existence and ecce-sistence.

There is a formal distinction between the two contractions. So it can easily seem that Hopkins confuses them when what he says seems to imply that a contraction of the continuous predicative kind can as it were grow ('as if my eye were still growing')[13] into a contraction concentrated upon the existence of the essence. This appearance is encouraged by his not being as focused as Scotus is on making logical and ontological distinctions, and by his frequent embedding of these in genealogical or etymological descriptions – which however are also ontological ones in so far as they are understood as being about being, which for Hopkins, agreeing with the later Scotus and disagreeing with Aristotle and Aquinas and Henry of Ghent, is univocal.

The suspicion that Hopkins persists in confusing the two kinds of contraction could be the consequence of the reader's failure to mark the difference between distinction and real separation and to grasp that when it is maintained of two items that they are formally distinct but therefore really inseparable this realness or 'realty' holds for both their existence and their essence. If it looks as though Hopkins is imagining the compressing of a predicated property to the point where predicativity suddenly ceases and gives way to existence, this may be because we are forgetting that the possibility of real existence is already on the scene with predicativity, and that essence remains on the scene still when the transition to existence is made. In other words, because the terms of the formal distinction are already concretely together in human experience, there is in reality no transition.

But in phenomenology there may be. There may be a switch from an experience of something in the world as the bearer of a universal or a common nature to an experience of it not simply as an individual determined by a specific differentiating predicate that may be instantiated by another particular and as such replaceable individual, but as an individual experienced as existing in its incommunicable irreplaceable thisness independently of its nature. Hopkins is an expert at describing, expressing and provoking experiences of the first sort, but he is simultaneously a specialist in evoking experiences of the second kind, a specialist in leading the reader to think of the things or persons invoked in a poem in their a-specific, unique singularity. The person in the poem may be himself, as in the poem 'My own heart let me have pity on . . .' It may be 'Christ our Lord' addressed in 'The Windhover'. It may be the windhover itself. Whatever be the being in question, whatever its what, Hopkins addresses it in its to-be. But at the same time in its not-to-be. He is a master – nay, servant – of the vulnerability of things, not least his own isolation, uniqueness, solitude, *Einsamkeit*, whatever we call it.

We might call it 'peculiarity'. This word could stand for the idiosyncratic seeming or strangeness or 'quaintance' Hopkins aims to convey in his poetry. On the other hand 'peculiarity' could stand for 'priviness' and ontological uniqueness that distinguishes a thing not as a quantified particular in virtue of its character but in virtue of its a-characterological existence. Existence brings with it the thought of inexistence. The thought of, for example, Binsey poplars, 'felled, felled, all felled' (1879), the thought of

> How to kéep [. . .]
> Back beauty, keep it, beauty, beauty, beauty . . . from vanishing away?

This is the thought of the fleetingness of inscapes that is never far away in the collection of poems by Hopkins for which Bridges could have borrowed from a collection of his own poems the title Testament of Beauty.

That is to say, the word 'peculiarity' presides over a real confusion, a confusion *a parte rei* the implications of which, we suggested, are overlooked by Peirce. They are not overlooked however by Hopkins. Despite our having just presented his seeming confusion in the temporal language of generation, creation, becoming and 'being doing', this apparent confusion is also an issue of ontology and logic. It is an issue of logic or 'logic' to the point that the principle of formal distinction is nearly tautological, as when it is exemplified by Scotus' proposition, 'Existence is really the same as essence', '*esse* est idem realiter cum *essentia*',[14] if this is interpreted as Scotus intended. The adverb 'really' in this sentence is not a cosmetic flourish. It could be replaced by a phrase like 'in concrete reality' in which the noun refers to things, *res*, and the adjective 'concrete' refers to a composition. The things put together in this case are existence and essence. So Scotus' proposition as a whole is a near-tautology affirming that the things put together are put together. What saves his proposition from being a pure tautology is the fact that the togetherness it affirms is real as contrasted with abstract, intellectual, conceptual or rational only. The sameness referred to in the *idem* of Scotus' proposition is real inseparability, not sameness of meaning. If it were the latter we should be faced with a full tautology, not an informative metaphysical truth. This is why the principle of formal distinction is a near-tautology. To say that two items are really and concretely inseparable is not yet to say that they are formally distinct. Furthermore, to say that Scotus seems to have anticipated Leibniz's distinction between truths of reason and truths of fact is not to say that for Scotus truths of reason are vacuous tautologies. They may be postcursors of Augustine's intuited truths and precursors of the intuitive propositions Reid calls principles of common sense.[15]

A formal distinction is neither purely real nor purely ideal or logical. It is intermediate between these possibilities or, rather, it straddles them. Hence the comparability of its status with that of a synthetic a priori statement. Synthetic a priori statements are a challenge to our simple ways of conceiving the distinction between the inside and the outside. They challenge us to ask ourselves whether the contingent and the necessary are simultaneously inside and outside each other. A similar inter- and intra-relationship is hinted at by formal distinction, except that where synthetic a priority purports to be a feature of certain statements (e.g. 'Every event has a cause'), formal distinction as understood by Scotus and Hopkins is an ontological feature of certain facts. This contrast of statement and fact is itself put into question by the formal distinction implicit or explicit in 'Existence is really the same as essence.' For its necessity, turning on the adverb 'really', appears to be that of a plain tautology, therefore one that is not stated but shown. Yet at the same time and by dint of the same adverb it purports to affirm a metaphysical fact. This contrast of stating and fact stated is put into question also by the contrast between the constatively propositional and the performatively pro-positional, where the pro-positional is understood as a proposal such as is brought into existence, other things being equal, by someone's uttering a sentence of the form 'I (hereby) propose . . .' What takes place in the utterance of such a sentence is a contraction between logical and ontological space. 'Contraction', we have seen, is a pregnant word. It gives birth to twinned meanings: to tightening as a natural phenomenon and to agreement as a legal and, Hopkins might have said, 'inlaw' event whose being-doing is cultural but at the same time natural for beings of the kind we call human.[16]

10
Being as Doing

Hopkins' hyphenation of being and doing gets some support from the fact that, as Heidegger reminds his readers, *Sein*, Being, is a verbal-noun. This reminder gives continual support to his exegesis in the *Introduction to Metaphysics* of Sophocles' *Antigone* because that exegesis is embedded in an exegesis of Parmenides' teaching that being and thinking are inseparable. Furthermore, rather as the philosophical thinking of Parmenides stands behind Heidegger's exegesis of Sophocles' poetry, a philosophical reflection on Parmenides' teaching stands behind the writing of Hopkins' poems. This holds chronologically in the sense that most of his poems were composed after, as an undergraduate at Oxford in the 1860s, he had composed the short essay on Parmenides. It holds also thematically in the sense that notions which are expressed in that essay, written before he had read Scotus, emerge in some of his poems and later prose. One such poem is 'As kingfishers catch fire' (1882). This includes the lines:

> Each mortal thing does one thing and the same:
> Deals out that being indoors each one dwells;
> Selves – goes itself, *myself* it speaks and spells;
> Crying *What I dó is me: for that I came.*

The first of these lines and the reference to being in the second hark back to the statement in Hopkins' essay on Parmenides that 'Parmenides will say that the mind's grasp – *noein*, the foreshadowing act – that this is blood or that blood is red is to be looked for in Being, the foredrawn, alone, not in the thing we named blood or the blood we worded as being red.' To this Hopkins adds the gloss: '"*phatisesthai*" is to "give it a name", to come out with something, to word or put a thought or thing'.[1] This notion of 'putting a thought or thing' and the affirmation of the 'simple *yes*'

(Hopkins' emphasis) of Being in the exegesis of Parmenides recur in the Comments on *The Spiritual Exercises* of St Ignatius Loyola in the statement that 'pitch is ultimately simple positiveness'.² Positiveness is posedness or putness, something's having been set (*gesetzt*), as in a proposition (a *Satz*). It is also opposedness to the negativity of the account defended by Henry of Ghent which Scotus rejects on the grounds that an independent explanatory principle of the individuality of a thing must be something positive, so cannot be due, as maintained by Henry, to the twin negations of the thing's not being another thing and its not being subdivided in the way of a heap. In the wake of both Parmenides and Scotus, Hopkins maintains that 'being differs from and is more than nothing, and not-being, and it is with precision expressed by the English *do*, the simple auxiliary'.

Hence the stressed and italicised '*dó*' in the fourth line of the poem 'As kingfishers catch fire . . .' This, taken in conjunction with 'being' in the second line, is a trace of the thought expressed in the Comments on Loyola that where non-personal things 'behave' (shudder-quotes), persons *do*. That is their *Seinsweise*, the way of their being. Hopkins endeavours to show this by proposing the barbarism 'doing-be' derived from the familiar syntax according to which we move from a simple statement like 'he said' to the emphatic form of the auxiliary verb in 'he did say' or of the corresponding Welsh '*Efe a ddywedodd* . . .' ('He it was who said . . .') which we have seen that Hopkins also gives.³ 'Doing-be' captures some of the flavour of 'Be-*ing*', *Sein*, understood as a verbal noun, 'a verb dancing at the centre of a noun'. The dance describes a circular movement in which the gyration around each other of the verb and the noun is at the same time the relationship of being to being-there, to *Da-sein* as analysed by Heidegger in the *Daseinsanalytik* of *Being and Time*. But, in the Comments on Loyola, Hopkins broaches his own (briefer) *Daseinanalytik*. It is an analysis of his own ownness. This is the ownness that cannot be the object of a gesture of pointing to a thing nearby or to oneself and-or attempting to identify it by referring to it as 'this'. This referring to it as 'this' is the indication of an entity of which one wishes to 'come out with' something said that makes room (*Da*) for what philosophers glibly call self-reference. In the lines cited above from 'As kingfishers catch fire . . .' Hopkins reconstrues the noun 'self' as verbal selving. This paraphrase is imitated when he spells *haecceitas* as *ecceitas*, thereby accentuating the addressive, imperative and performative-productive force of the visibly if not audibly abbreviated form of the Latin word, turning it into the equivalent of the call to attention 'Look' either of another's call for help or of my 'Here I am; send me' (Isaiah 6: 8).

Let us respond to this call to attention by looking again at some of the sentences on the first of the nine pages on which Hopkins carries out his analysis of selftaste, nine pages that lead up to his re-inscaping of *haecceitas* as *ecceitas*.

On the last of those nine pages he concludes his argument as follows: '(3) The third alternative then follows. I am due to an extrinsic power.' The abruptness with which he announces this inference is reminiscent of Scotus' method of disputation and literary style, for instance in the elimination of alternatives we saw Scotus carrying out in his analyses of the various accounts of the so-called principle of individuation summarised above in Chapter 4. Hopkins first disposes of the argument that his coming into being could have been a matter of chance. Incidentally touching on the distinction between chaos and cosmos that we shall mention again below, he writes: 'The most plausible, if anything is plausible here, is that virgin matter is due to chance, other things not.' Then he rules out the possibility that he could have brought himself into existence, giving special attention to the hypothesis attributed to 'the Averrhoists . . . the Hegelians and others' that he might be indistinguishable from the universal mind or being itself. To entertain that hypothesis, he adds in parentheses, would be 'to assume in one-self a hypostatic union'.

A propos of hypostatic unions, in the course of a discussion of formal distinction David Armstrong writes: 'Scotus gave as a model the simultaneous unity and distinguishability of the members of the Holy Trinity, a model which had power to silence objectors in his own day but is unfortunately unavailable to me.'[4] The general problem touched on in this remark will be taken up in our next chapter. Another specific example of it is very pertinent to the question how closely the layout of Hopkins' analysis corresponds to that of the analysis of formal distinction conducted by Scotus in the various places where he discusses formal distinction and individuality. Of these places we should naturally expect the most relevant for the purpose of this book to be found in the parts treating those topics in the Venice edition of Scotus' works that Hopkins came across in the Baddeley library at St Mary's Hall, Stonyhurst, in 1872, namely *Ordinatio*, that is to say the reviewed text, also referred to as *Scriptum Oxoniense* or *Opus Oxoniense* or simply *Oxoniense*. There is no mention there, however, of the word *haecceitas*! The notion but not the word is to be found there (at lib. II. d. 3 n. 1–6), but for the use of the term itself one has to look to the *Reportatio Parisiensia*, lib. II. d. 12. q. 5 n. 1. 8. 13. 14. and the *Quaestiones Subtilissimae in Metaphysicam Aristotelis*, lib. VII. q. 13 n. 9. 26. One also has to assume that Hopkins encountered the word in conversation with colleagues and friends, in particular such fellow Scotists as his journal for 1874 records him meeting: 'I walked with Henry Lucas by the river and talked Scotism with him for the last time.'[5] 'I met Mr David Lewis, a great Scotist.'[6]

Of course it must not be overlooked that any comments we now go on to make about that other would-be Scotist Gerard Manley Hopkins will be comments on his Comments on *The Spiritual Exercises* of St Ignatius Loyola. Even so, in describing a remark as a comment we grant ourselves the freedom to range widely, as widely as, in the present case, to read Scotus' text in terms of Ignatius' and vice versa. The reader will decide how strong a case has been made for doing that, for instance for interpreting Hopkins' first title in a way that guides our understanding both of Ignatius and of Scotus. The title is 'On *Principium sive Fundamentum*'. Ignatius himself says, '*Principle* looks rather to theory, *Foundation* to practice.' And in so far as *theōria* is looking, it is already in part *praxis*. That this is so is endorsed by Scotus' chiasmic conception of the relation between intellect and will. It is endorsed also by Hopkins' hyphenation of the hyphenation of being and doing with Parmenides' hyphenation of being and *noein* (thinking, judging, perception, grasping, *Begriff*).

In the course of our chapter on Hopkins' comments on Parmenides it was pointed out that the borrowing from Ignatius in the heading of the comments on the latter is followed immediately by another borrowing: 'Homo creatus est'. So it is with the orders of creation that we are concerned in the concluding section of this chapter, especially with the order in which these orders are treated by Scotus and Hopkins. Before passing to that, however, mention must be made of a difficulty that connects with what might seem to be implied by Hopkins' agreement with both Scotus and Ignatius that *theōria* and principle have a foundation in *praxis*. I am put under an obligation to mention this difficulty by the declaration made in the opening sentence of the preceding chapter that I was hoping to make at least one small step for non-human and human kind. Indeed, throughout the entirety of this book I entertain the hope that Hopkins, helped by Scotus, is a fellow-traveller with me on that path. But it is difficult to see how Hopkins can be that if he agrees with what he is told by his religion and his Saint, namely that, in the latter's words:

> Man was created to praise, reverence, and serve God our Lord, and by this means to save his soul; and the other things on the face of the earth were created for man's sake, and in order to aid him in the prosecution of the end for which he was created ... It is therefore necessary that we should make ourselves indifferent to all created things ...[7]

Indifferent? The sentence in which this word occurs here could be read as an encapsulation of what caused the young priest-poet Hopkins so much anxiety that he destroyed most of the poetry he had written up until then. So more work than I am qualified to undertake has to be done on the grammar of the hyphen that connects and-or disconnects the poet and the priest. As for the word 'indifferent', the Fiery Saint himself helps us to escape a too crude interpretation of it when he goes on to specify that we should make ourselves indifferent

> ... in such sort that we do not for our part wish for health rather than sickness, for wealth rather than poverty, for honour rather than sickness, for a long life rather than a short one, and so in all other things, desiring and choosing only that which leads us more directly to the end for which we were created.

In such sort that we will not to will either alternative of these pairs of contraries, whether to will not to will is, as here, to will that 'Thy will be done on earth as it is in heaven', or whether it is construed as the letting-be of the moment of which Dennis Potter says that in it 'Things are both more trivial than they ever were, and more important than they ever were, and the difference between the trivial and the important doesn't seem to matter.' Either of these construals would open a way that prevents Ignatius' words 'to save his soul' from leaving in one's mouth the nasty taste of the thought that the one above all for whom this salvation matters most is oneself. Where the self in question is Gerard Manley Hopkins this aftertaste can be prevented from contaminating his selftaste only if in seeking himself he can find a way consistent with loyalty to Loyola of understanding that 'the difference between the trivial and the important doesn't seem to matter'. How can we expect him to succeed in finding such a way that is consistent with his saying 'I find myself . . . more important to myself than anything I see'?

The comparative 'more important' raises again the question posed in the paragraphs treating of 'peculiarity' in the previous chapter where we observed that this word can refer either to a property that admits of degrees or to a subject or object that is a bearer of properties. It is this question that is raised again in the first part of Hopkins' Comments on *The Spiritual Exercises*. His 'more' signals that he has in mind what Scotus would call 'common natures', accidental or necessary characteristics of something or somebody. He also employs in one and the same sentence the expressions 'more distinctive' and 'incommunicable'. The first of these expressions alludes to the communicable, that is to say sharable properties of things or persons, what their nature allows them to possess in common. 'Incommunicable', on the other hand, is Scotus' word for an entity's individuality, precisely that in which it is distinct from (non-identical with) all other individuals though not on account of its predicates. This latter distinctiveness is an absolute difference. So care must be taken to distinguish these two senses, but also to recognise the peculiarity of the 'relation' between them. The peculiarity of this peculiarity is that it reaches beyond the semantic and syntactic strangenesses encountered in Hopkins' works and illustrated in citations from them made in the course of this study. It extends to how these uncommon common natures address themselves to us through singularities that never cease to be vulnerable to construal as no more or less than particularities. So there is the liability of inscapes to be only glimpsed, but there is also our liability to miss or only fleetingly sense the uniqueness of the individuals to which or to whom natures belong. Hopkins' bold stroke is to attempt to give his readers a glimpse of the quasi-relation between these two liabilities by rewriting Scotus' *haecceitas* as *ecceitas*.

It would be too extreme a defence of Hopkins as exponent of Scotism to suppose him to be imagining a reversal of Marx's conception of a conversion of the quantitative into the qualitative: to suppose that the graduated and other qualities collected in a common nature with its less than numerical unity become numbers when the carrier of those qualities gains a numerical unity concomitant with its individuality. Admittedly, this defence would chime with the fact that intrinsic to Hopkins' poetics is number as rhythm and musical measure. It would chime too with the fact that hints are heard throughout his work as to how his poetics might be developed into a cosmology. However, this, like any other 'quantitist' defence, would be too high a price to pay for the achievement of an account of the determinate individuality of material substance. If, inspired perhaps by Pythagoras or Plato's *Timaeus*, Hopkins thought such an account could be based on the idea that each item in the natural number series is unique, he would be forgetting that in Question Four of *De Principio Individuationis* Scotus denies this possibility in the objections he makes to the analyses of individuality given (by, for example, Giles of Rome and Godfrey of Fontaines) in terms of quantity, as was noted above in our fourth chapter. He rolls out a panoply of objections, many of them appealing overtly to the authority of Aristotle. One of these objections is that to suppose quantity can be the factor responsible for the determinate individuality of a material substance is to demand an answer to the question what gives determinate individuality to quantity. Another of his objections is that to hold that an accident can be the cause of the determinate individuality of a material substance is to infringe the standard Scholastic rules governing levels of causal eminence.

These and the other objections made to the half-dozen or so Questions considered in Scotus' treatise on the principle of individuation are objections to accounts pretending to explain how one or another version of that principle could be responsible for the determinate individuation of material substance. He is treating, roughly speaking, of what Hopkins is referring to when on the first page of his Comments he mentions the visible world, 'anything I see', 'the world without'. This is the world, he says, that

Being as Doing

is 'commonly dwelt on'. And, as we have just observed, this is the world to which almost the entirety of Scotus' Six Questions on Individuation is devoted.

On the other hand, what almost the entirety of Hopkins' Comments on Ignatius dwells on is what the former would describe as the inscapes of the world within, 'that being indoors each one dwells', the ways of being and doing, of being as doing the cataloguing of which he resumes under the remark that all these are 'more important to myself than anything I see'.

This is not a statement about what is more important in general. It is either a statement about things that are objectively more important 'to myself', or one about himself declaring that he rates these things more highly than 'anything I see'. The myself who makes this statement is the Hopkins of circa 1881. Taking his 'anything I see' as meaning the visible world, we may be appalled at the thought of the strain and stress he must have experienced through being simultaneously torn in one direction by such a downgrading of the world of the senses, including presumably the world of music, and torn in the opposite direction by the spontaneous desire to sing the praises of the natural world regarded as embraced by the possible Cinderella Transcendental about which we expressed some misgivings in Chapter 6.

A year after he began his reflections on *The Spiritual Exercises,* in a letter dated 2 November 1881 to the Anglican Canon R.W. Dixon that lends itself to being regarded as a postscript to those reflections, Hopkins writes:

> This I say: my vocation puts before me a standard so high that a higher can be found nowhere else . . . A purpose may look smooth and perfect from without but frail and faltering from within. I have never wavered in my vocation, but I have not lived up to it. I destroyed the verse I had written when I entered the Society . . .[8]

He leaves the reader of his letter in no doubt as to which vocation is meant. And the reader of this study should be left in no doubt that in the name of a certain logico-rhetorological chiasmic Crux that is distinct from though not inseparable from a theology of the Cross (so by definition not in a relation of *distinctio formalis* with that theology), the present study too lends its ear to a certain vocation. This vocation, described by the author of this study in detail in other studies and largely assumed in this study, is the religious or 'religious' though not necessarily and not necessarily not religioned calling that addresses us apocalyptically as though both from 'the world within' and from 'the world without' in the voice of that practical *scientia* we name conscience that is distinct but really inseparable from human consciousness (so by definition in a relation of *distinctio formalis* with it).

Further, the word 'destroyed' in Hopkins' letter should remind the reader of this study of those places where Hopkins gives voice to lamentations like

> The ashtree growing in the corner of the garden was felled. It was lopped first: I heard the sound and looking out and seeing it maimed there came at that moment a great pang and I wished to die and not to see the inscapes of the world destroyed any more.[9]

Such destruction is in all probability a manifestation of deafness in the first place to the call made by the sheer existence of each existent, whether of the world within or of the world without or of the world outwith this opposition. The world outwith this opposition is, in a broad sense of the adjectives, a world of ethical and religious vocation. It is not a world facing us with a choice between two cities. It is a world that is numerically one, an universe in which the city of God is not another place or time, but a metaphor of the adverbiality of a strange new way of being a citizen of this world here and now that makes room not only for citizens but also for love of the singular ash tree, Binsey poplars, the tree on which Christ was crucified, Dennis Potter's blossomest plum tree and all the other 'common natures' revealed in their ipsissimal signate singularity as sung in Hopkins' poems and sealed in Scotus' metaphysical notion of formal distinction.

As well as being the author of a tale of two cities and of two kinds of love, Augustine is the source of a notion of intuition that inspires Scotus' and Hopkins' thinking of what the latter, on the first page of his 'Analytic of Dasein', refers to as 'the mind . . . when I consider my selfbeing'. In that thinking Hopkins remains very much within the circling of his selving, considering himself to have responded in his poems to the call to celebrate his responsibility to 'the external world'. The latter is the world on the metaphysics of which Scotus concentrates in his own account of what Ignatius will call the '*Principium sive Fundamentum*' of individuation. But we can no longer abstain from observing that this account, although ostensibly directed at an analysis of the individuality of material substance, is embedded between two documents both of which treat of the individuality and other metaphysical features of certain immaterial beings, the ones that in religious traditions are called angels! That is, we find ourselves back with a problem emanating from the same source as the one with which we saw David Armstrong was anxious not to get himself involved. We find ourselves therefore with an obligation to make up our minds regarding these problems and their source as they pose themselves in more general terms. An attempt to meet this obligation will be made in the next chapter.

In the present chapter it has gradually emerged that we have been engaged in attempting to establish a correspondence among three provisionalities: the provisionality of the *Daseinsanalytik* that is conducted in *Being and Time*, the provisionality of what we have referred to as the Analytic of Dasein carried out in the first nine or so pages of Hopkins' account of the special status accorded there by him to his own selfness, and, thirdly, the provisionality of Scotus' pages on the so-called principle of individuation. We have just drawn attention to the way what is said on those pages is subservient to the metaphysical and theological discussions of the personality of incorporeal beings less than the divine and more than human that furnish the point of the pages on the principle of individuation which concentrate on corporeal beings.

No more than Armstrong in his researches will we in ours be concerned with angels. As for the Analytic of Dasein in *Being and Time*, Heidegger warns us explicitly that it looks forward from the analysis of the structures of selfhood to promised descriptions of Being as such. Here and there he implies that these descriptions of Being as such will improve our understanding of beings. In Hopkins the order of proceeding is reversed. His Analytic only mentions beings in the exterior world on its way to what becomes its predominant interest, human beings, above all himself. Properly understood in the light of the warning cited from John Burnet, the topic of his essay on the poem of Parmenides is not Being but beings, τα ὄντα.

11
From Method of Ignorance to Way of Love

Under the spell of Hopkins, who was under the spell of Scotus, I have in the foregoing pages made much of the way in which the first of these writers alters the spelling of *haecceitas* to *ecceitas*. I have made much also of the tie that both of these authors see between this Latin word or these Latin words and the notion of being as existence. For although, as argued by Scotus against Giles of Rome,[1] existence is not necessarily the cause or ground of thisness, thisness may entail existence. This tie led me to a further connection, that of existence and the goodness of its existence for each existent, whether or not the existent can itself express the claim to existence that is grounded on the goodness for the existent of its existence or depends on other existents to speak or to imagine themselves speaking as advocates on its behalf.

My responsibility to speak for existents as such does not exclude my responsibility towards what might be considered not to fall within the category of existents, for instance the unborn, the dead, spectres or ghosts, reference to which we might think it necessary to qualify with the conditional clause 'if there be any such thing(s)', or 'if there were any such thing(s)'. This is a conditional clause with which many people would want to qualify any reference to God or G-D or a god. These people would include those who would experience difficulty reading a study of Scotus and Hopkins which, like this one, makes only passing reference to Divinity. Both Scotus and Hopkins are so committed to a metaphysics of God, existence and salvation that there would appear to be no viable route from such a metaphysics to the universes of discourse inhabited by the modern, postmodern or post-postmodern authors whose work is placed alongside that of Scotus and Hopkins in the chapters of this study.

The thought of this dilemma drove me close to abandoning my project.

Casting around for a methodology that would legitimate my not giving up my purpose, I first bethought myself of the way by which Levinas postpones his theological reflections until he has expounded his humanism of the other human being. But I was unable to reach a point from which I could see clearly how what he calls his *Théologies* could be continuous with the theology that supported and was supported by the philosophical thinking of Scotus and Hopkins, let alone how their philosophical thinking was to be supported by the diaphanous remnant of religious faithfulness which was all I myself could manage to muster in place of faith in a religion.[2]

Then Levinas came to my rescue from a new direction. Before describing how that happened I shall describe the method of willed ignorance I considered adopting before I decided that it was too arbitrarily wilful. That method, flirted with in the hope that it would enable me to carry on writing a non-theological book about two theologians, has a theological origin, as too does the resource on which I then drew in the hope that it would give direction to my philosophical hitch-hike.

A third theologian, Nicholas of Cusa, writes:

> Nothing could be more beneficial for even the most zealous searcher for knowledge than his being in fact most learned in that very ignorance which is peculiarly his own; and the better a man will have known his own ignorance, the greater his learning will be. It is in bearing this in mind that I have undertaken the risk of writing a few words on learned ignorance.[3]

On the one hand, ignorance is a state, the state of lacking knowledge. Ignorance as a state is denoted by a noun, the noun 'ignorance', so let us call it nominal or substantival ignorance. Although such ignorance, like the knowledge that would put an end to it, is a state, it is not a state of mind if by a state of mind we mean a psychological state in the way belief and doubt and suspicion and fear are states of mind. Such ignorance is a state of affairs appertaining to the mind without being a state of mind. Just as it is possible for me not to know that I know a certain thing, as when I do not believe that I know it or believe that I do not know it, it is possible for me not to know that I am ignorant of it, as when I do not believe that I am ignorant of it or believe that I am not ignorant of it. I can be in a state of ignorance about either my knowledge or my ignorance. Here agnotology is the mirror image of epistemology.

Nominal or substantival ignorance is to be distinguished from ignorance understood as marked primarily by a verb. Verbal or willed ignorance is what people display when they refuse to take notice of something or someone. It is operative ignorance. It is the deed or practice of refusing to have anything to do with someone or something: *bouder*, as French says, meaning to give the cold shoulder or to snub.

To ignore is a sign of not wanting to know. But it can be more. It can be a sign of wanting not to know. Both not wanting to know and wanting not to know may be signs of a suspension of curiosity. However, such suspension is not necessarily a sign of disrespect or indifference. A suspension of curiosity may be a sign of respect for someone's privacy. Again, we may prefer ignorance where we would find knowledge hard to bear, as when we switch off a television report of an atrocity either again out of a wish not to be intrusive or simply in order to avoid the pain that seeing the pictures would cause us.

Because such refusal is an act, it makes sense to ask after its motive, whatever its motive may be. On the other hand, of nominal ignorance, the state of not knowing, it does not obviously make sense to ask after its motive, though we might well ask after its cause. The cause of someone's ignorance might be the fact that she or he had not attended a school, had been brought up in a house without books in it, or had lived a sheltered life. However, the explanation for someone's ignorance of a certain thing may be traceable to a more or less conscious refusal by the person concerned to inquire. It may be unclear whether the explanation of this refusal should be the giving of a cause or the giving of a motive. Motives may be mixed. Also, in particular circumstances motives may be difficult to distinguish from causes. This may be because we have not decided whether we are inquiring as physiologists or as psychologists. It may be because we are confused over how the hyphen is to be interpreted in the expression 'psycho-physiology'. It may be because we are puzzled over how a patient can be regarded ('treated') as both a person and a case for treatment. However, despite the difficulty as to how these questions are to be answered in particular circumstances, no difficulty seems to be presented by the general conceptual contention that, since nominal ignorance is a state, it can be explained by the giving of a cause, and that if we think explaining it will involve the giving of a motive this can only be if we are thinking of a verbal ignoring that led to the nominal ignorance, a refusal to inquire leading to the state of absence of knowledge.

The absent knowledge just referred to may be what Bertrand Russell called knowledge by acquaintance and what John Grote, in a book Hopkins read, called knowledge of acquaintance, that is to say knowledge as knowing a thing or a person.[4] On the other hand, the absent knowledge may be what Russell called knowledge by description, description of a state of affairs, knowing that such and such, perhaps what Grote called knowledge of judgement.

In other contexts the absent knowledge in question may be a knowing-how. Knowing-how is neither a nominal or substantival ignorance nor a verbal ignorance. It is a practical ignorance that is not what could be called ignorance by non-acquaintance. Nor is it ignorance of a state of affairs, ignorance-that. To suppose that knowing-how is either of these is to evince a certain ignorance-how, to wit ignorance how to talk correctly. It is to confuse the mastery of a linguistic skill with the possession of an item of theoretical knowledge, for example with a grammarian's theoretical knowledge. The grammarian codifies the rules or practices that constitute a grammar. But if his or our understanding of what the grammarian formulates requires that there be a real or imaginary book of rules in terms of which his grammar is to be interpreted, we shall either have begun an infinite regress or begun a regress that comes to a halt because we are too tired to go on or because our time runs out. Such interpretation is necessary only where there has been a breakdown of communication analogous to a failure to translate correctly what someone speaking a foreign language has said to us. That is when we may need to consult a dictionary or a grammar book. Doing that presupposes a minimum of shared understanding, but this minimal understanding is the possession of a competence, not the possession of a piece of information against which we check what someone says. When Wittgenstein says that we follow rules blindly he does not mean that in following a rule of language there has to exist an object or objective of which we are blind, an alleged image or formula inscribed on the retina of the mind but which cannot be seen. To believe that this is what following a rule requires is to be victim to what Max Black dubbed the grammarian's fallacy. To follow a rule of grammar is to behave in a regular way without there having to be before our mind's eye a principle or idea or proposition that we have to interpret and apply whenever we make ourselves understood. Finding that we are understood is finding our regularities shared with those of our interlocutors.

The grammarian's fallacy is a fallacy because it exaggerates the importance of the proposition as the proposition is understood in traditional logic. The commission of it is encouraged even by that most perceptive of philosophical archaeologists R. G. Collingwood when he distinguishes relative presuppositions from absolute presupposition. For his way of using these expressions is liable to create the impression that he is distinguishing two kinds of proposition, whereas it is only relative presuppositions (for example 'The change of position of a hand on the dial of a barometer is caused by a change in atmospheric pressure') that are propositions defined as entities that may be true or false. Absolute presuppositions (for example 'All events have causes' or, at a later stage of scientific thinking, 'Only some events have causes') are precisely entities of which it makes no sense to predicate truth or falsity. They belong to the subconscious of scientific and other thinking. They go without saying. They are unquestioned. Rather than describing a state of affairs, they prescribe what can be questioned and answered. They function less like propositions or statements in the indicative mood than like principles which, if they weren't tacit, 'understood' in the sense of being taken for granted, would be expressed as imperatives – though note that the German word *Satz* translates both the English words 'principle' and 'statement' or 'proposition'.

It is because absolute presuppositions are implicit rather than explicit that they are able to set out the space within which questions as to the truth and falsity of statements may arise.

Is then an absolute presupposition something of which we are in absolute ignorance? Not if absoluteness of ignorance requires that it be something unknowable for all time. Under that requirement 'All events have causes' would be something of which our ignorance can be only relatively absolute, absolute relative to a certain historical span of thinking covering, say, the period from Newton to Einstein and quantum mechanics.

Hence, surprisingly, it is among the so-called 'timeless truths' of logic, say the principle of identity 'if p then p', that we should look for absolutely absolute ignorance. Timeless truths are not among what Collingwood would count as absolute presuppositions. Absolute presuppositions as described by him are not timeless truths, for he allows that absolute presuppositions can over time become relative. They are synthetic a priori. They are not tautologies or principles that lay down the analytic a priori form of tautologies. We are in relatively absolute ignorance of absolute presuppositions because they are hidden, but we are in absolutely absolute ignorance of tautologies because they are not hidden enough. If we understand them, they are not hidden enough to leave room for it to be asked whether they are true. The very of-courseness adverted to in the exclamation 'Of course it is true that if p then p' is a mark of there being no room in logic to ask whether it is true, hence whether it is something we can know. Thus, saying that we can be in absolute ignorance of the truth value of a tautology is not an admission of our not knowing. It is not the sort of thing that we can logically claim to know, so it is not the sort of thing of which it can be claimed that we do not know it. Or rather, it is not the sort of thing of which it can be claimed that we are in the sort of ignorance in which we may be when we do not know what causes the level of the mercury to rise in a certain instrument. However, that sort of knowledge and ignorance is not the only sort of knowledge and ignorance. It may well be the case that claims to such knowledge or non-knowledge are made by people for whom the so-called truths of logic go without saying and which, because there is no conceivable ground for doubt in their case, leave no room for claims to know them. That is something about which there can be confidence.

Confidence, however, is not the same as truth. Even so-called timeless truths of logic are open to a historicity analogous to that of absolute presuppositions. For even tautologies may not be obvious to those who are learning to talk or beginning to think. And there is a sense in which the adult too is a learner, a sense in which the adult may learn something from the infant, on pain of one's claim to be judged a mature adult being challenged. The child is father of the man. The mature adult has learned with difficulty a trick that comes naturally and easily to the child. This is the trick of applying prospectively the lesson acquired retrospectively that habitually absolute presuppositions have the habit of turning into relative ones, and that even an apparently timeless tautological truth that passes for an orthodox logical tautology is imaginably revisable. That is to say, following a responsible method or way calls for the application of verbal willed ignorance to nominal ignorance. The state of being unknowable as determined by a currently entrenched pattern of seeing the world is an unknowability and therefore an ignorance that we ought not 'want to know'. It is an ignorance with which we ought to have nothing to do, an ignorance we should ignore. But in order to ignore it we must take note of it. Put simply, the order 'Ignore this' is an order that cannot be unreservedly obeyed. We disobey this order in obeying it. Therefore, if to anatomise is to dissect, the act of ignoring which we have called verbal ignorance cannot be anatomised. It cannot be absolved from itself. It is never absolute.

Furthermore, if only because it is not barbarous to say 'I hereby constate' or 'I hereby perform', the performative act of speech cannot be separated from the constative act. They are inseparable but in Scotus' sense of the words, formally distinct. This is a corollary of the formal distinction that holds according to him between will and intellect. Nor can verbal ignorance be separated absolutely from nominal ignorance (and indeed these two inseparabilities are inseparable from each other), for the immediate consequence of an act of ignoring is that something is in a state of having been ignored. Except that here again what is ignored is simultaneously brought before our attention, not ignored, not subjected to the attitude between attentiveness and deliberate neglect that we ordinarily call indifference.

Further, although, as noted, the refusal to take heed of something may be an act of disrespect, it may be an act of respect. It may be a refusal to intrude. It may be a letting something be, a letting that is paradigmatically middle-voiced. That is to say, it may be neither only in the active voice nor only in the passive voice, but in both or neither at one and the same time or in turns.

The middle-voiced or medial diathesis is a voice that calls for a patient listening that, when we actively ignore something, allows what is thereby also nominally ignored to speak for itself. Both right-brained and left-brained, both *yin* and *yang*, unanatomisable ignorance is a *docta ignorantia*, a learned and learning ignorance, hence a promising hope for the increase of knowledge and understanding on the one hand and responsivity and justice(s) on the other. For what we have been saying in these paragraphs and what we have earlier found Hopkins saying about the connection between inscape and instress amount to saying that these two hands cooperate.

The emollient tone of the sentences that end the immediately preceding paragraph softens to some degree the violence of the silent assent that Hopkins, in the wake of Scotus, gives to a wilful verbal ignorance regarding what may seem to be the answer they should give to the question, left unanswered by them both, as to what causes the individuation of an entity. What was described as a plain and tautological explanation was given in Chapter 9 of why they left this question unanswered. It was conceded, however, that the question and the answer connect with questions left unanswered out of educated verbal ignorance in the tradition of so-called negative theology. And Scotus himself writes, *Ratio ultima [intima] haecceitatis non est quaerenda nisi in divina voluntate*, 'The ground of this ultimate [intimate] *haecceitas* is not to be sought otherwise than in the divine will.'[5] Hopkins agrees.

The only honest way for anyone who disagrees with them to meet their arguments for holding this is to argue back. This is what in Chapter 4 we saw Scotus himself doing in response to the philosophers and theologians who took a different view from his about the cause of singularity. For instance, one might argue that the principle of sufficient reason is insufficient. What, one may ask, is so compelling about the idea that nothing can come from nothing, and that what there is must have had a cause? In the *Timaeus* Plato gets by with a notion of creation that is not a creation *ex nihilo*. Ockham holds that difficulties stand in the way of Scotus' attempts to prove the impossibility of an infinite series of productive as distinguished from conservative causes.[6] And the physicists' Big Bang is a beginning of order, not a beginning of chaotic stuff. Their word for the world is 'cosmos', a whole that is ordered, as (to move from physics to metaphysics) Being is essentially ordered according to Scotus. True, physicists' answers to cosmological questions may not be answers to metaphysical questions, let alone to theological ones. But from none of these fields does one learn why the idea of a beginning of whatever there is makes more sense than the idea that whatever there is has no beginning. The latter idea seems to me to be at least as persuasive as the former.

I found myself (to vary Hopkins' words) unable to adopt an attitude of active ignorance to one of these ideas rather than to the other. I had therefore to continue my search until I remembered Levinas' admission that although he was tempted to give more prominence than he does in his doctrine of responsibility to the word 'love', he refrained from doing so because he believed the power of that word had become adulterated (*galvaudé*) by, for instance, becoming tinged by the self-love with which it is associated in following the precept to love one's neighbour as oneself. Levinas' avowal alerted me to a strategy not of avoidance, but of voidance, a recourse to the spoiled word in order to empty it of the accretions considered to be unwelcome. It seems unlikely that those disposable unwelcome accretions would include the honesty mentioned a few moments ago understood as a readiness to allow that one's own absolute presuppositions might be only relative ones. Allowing that might well be considered to be part of what is meant by the precept to love one's neighbour as oneself.

Furthermore, it so happens that this strategy of disinfective *kenōsis* as a way of avoiding the theological difficulties I find myself incompetent to tackle would not be severed altogether from theology, not anyway from the theology that proclaims that God is Love. The recipe I thought I might follow would take this proclamation seriously. It would take it as seriously as it is taken when the word 'Love' stands in for the word 'God' in the poem which Hopkins loved best of all those by George Herbert, and as it is taken in the poem composed by Hopkins himself which begins with the plea

Let me be to Thee as the circling bird

and ends by announcing that

I have found the dominant of my range and state –
Love, O my God, to call Thee Love and Love.

But precisely which word in this sonnet by Hopkins concerning music and singing sounds the dominant note and which sounds the tonic? Herbert puts the word 'Love' in his poem wherever he could have put the word 'God', except that at just one such place in it he puts instead the word 'Lord', lest his reader fail to heed the Johannine equation of God and Love on which the poet wishes to draw. For untheists to heed that equation might be to discover themselves vested by it with the authority to regard as agapology what if regarded as theology they might find not to their 'self-taste'. More importantly, to heed that equation might be to remove what such unbelievers or disbelievers would otherwise experience as a hindrance to their reading the writings of Hopkins or Scotus or this book about them. To such reluctant readers I simply say: *ecce*, try reading these writings in the light of the lesson George Herbert's 'Love (III)' translates from 1 John 4: 8,16). Of course, such reluctant readers will simply respond that the rule of substitution I wish to pass on to them owes some of its authority to the scripture from which it is cited, and that therefore my subterfuge does not get them or myself off the theological hook. They would be right to respond in this way, just as it would be right to say by analogy that the only test of the authority of Aristotle – whom Duns and his contemporaries single out by conferring on him the emphatically definite description 'The Philosopher' – can be our engaging in philosophical discussion as freely as possible with these authors and my reluctant readers, however amateurishly. The authority of The Church and its theologians or philosophers, not least Aristotle, can be tested only by engaging in theological discussion with them, however amateurishly. Not only in theological or philosophical discussion, but also out of regard for these scholars as beings endowed with the human nature we share with them and out of respect for the individuality by which we are as distinct from each other as, in the letter addressed to Bridges cited in Chapter 2, Hopkins writes that he is from that friend: 'most determined and distinctive, at pitch', as distinctive as he finds himself to be in the inexhaustible 'self-discovery' passage cited in Chapter 4.

Hear how the resolve not to be so self-deprecatingly hard on himself reached by one of the interlocutors in the last lines of Herbert's poem is replicated in the sonnet composed in Dublin by Hopkins during the *annus terribilis* of 1885. In the first quatrain the poet asks to be weaned from self-hate.

> My own heart let me more have pity on; let
> Me live to my sad self hereafter kind,
> Charitable; not live this tormented mind
> With this tormented mind tormented yet.

The reader of these lines should remember that in the gospel according to Hopkins *caritas* is intimately bound up with doing in the way, according to his onto-praxeology, being and doing are bound up with each other and thereby, however remotely, with the transcendental notion that Plato called *to agathon*, the good.

12

Categories and Transcendentals Transcended

Agathology and agapology. In turning our attention now to the relationship between these two spheres we turn our attention to attention itself, attention 'as such'.

Attention is a counterweight to intention. Intention is exercised in the directedness both of conscious understanding to its object and of the will to its proximate or remote end. These directings are interdependent. Correcting what he sees as the prejudice in favour of the speculative manifested in Aristotle and Thomism, Scotus argues that the will acts in the light of knowledge furnished by the understanding, whereas knowledge furnished by the understanding depends on the will for its application. Furthermore, Scotus argues, and Hopkins chimes in, the will can will the positively infinite, whereas the understanding has to make do with the negativity of the not-finite.

How, however, can Scotus maintain this interdependence of understanding and will yet be described by Hannah Arendt as 'the lonely defender of the primacy of the Will over Intellect'?[1] One way to make this possible would be to interpret the thesis of interdependence as referring to the human understanding and the human will while interpreting the thesis of the primacy of the will as referring to the divine. God's will would be metaphysically prior because God is the Creator. This way of safeguarding consistency seems not to be accessible to the citizens of the city of the ungodly. And it is they who concern us here where we are attempting to demonstrate the direct relevance to the unbeliever and disbeliever – as such and not as a potential convert – of the works of Scotus and Hopkins despite the absolute presupposition of Christian theology to which the works of both of these authors subscribe. We have based the chief hope of demonstrating some degree of relevance on the premise that God is Love, acknowledging that this premise promises or threatens to reimport the theology implicit in its scriptural place of origin. To the acknowledgement of that origin should be added acknowledgement of the Augustinian element in the armoury drawn on by Scotus and Hopkins in their endeavour to 'correct' or at least 'colour' Aristotle and Aquinas, as Scotus admits he 'colours' Anselm's so-called ontological argument. Arendt reminds us of this element when, more than once, she cites the statement *amo: volo ut sis* apparently attributed to Augustine by Heidegger in a letter to her. She cites this as though it is affirmed or cited with approval by Scotus:

> The willing ego, when it says in its highest manifestation, '*Amo: Volo ut sis*', – and not 'I want to have you' or 'I want to rule you' – shows itself capable of the same love with which supposedly God loves men, whom He created only because He willed them to exist and whom He loves without desiring them.[2]

The following four comments on these remarks will help to explain how the latter relate to the groundplan of this study.

(1) Although the Latin assertion gets translated sometimes as 'I love: I want you to be as you are', this takes the '*ut*' twice over. I translate the Latin assertion as 'I love: I want you to be.'
(2) My translation is not only more economical; it also serves the assumption by which this study is enframed that a prima facie but significant ethical claim is founded on another's sheer existence, independently of that existent's first-level predicates.
(3) My translation also fits what I take to be the emphasis put by Scotus, followed by Hopkins, on ultimate existents as singulars.
(4) Although I have endorsed one of Arendt's translations of *volo*, as 'I want', I am attracted to the alternative 'I will' which she uses of God. He, the Creator, is said to have willed each individual to exist. No doubt he also wanted (or desired) each human being to exist, and would probably not have willed them to had he not wanted to. But whereas it is not altogether unclear what might be meant by the sentence 'I hereby will that you exist' (uttered for instance in a fairytale by a magician), it is quite unclear what could be meant by 'I hereby want you to exist.' Is this a 'Royal Want' like the 'Royal We' in terms of which Her Majesty proclaims it? In any case, her subjects lack the authority or power assumed by these odd locutions, and it is love generally, including love from or towards the powerless or underprivileged that we are aiming to explicate as *volo ut sis*.

The main purpose of the last of the four comments made above on the sentences cited from Arendt is to bring out that the possibility of translating her *volo* as will rather than want paves the way for the further notion we are about to take the opportunity to develop out of Scotus and apply to Hopkins, namely the notion of willing not to will. Only willing contrasted with wanting can be construed as an act or quasi-act that cancels a possibly intended act in order to make way for a passivity on the part of the agent.[3]

Arendt says that love is the self's highest manifestation. Despite this and despite her seeming confidence that Scotus would endorse her statement, he often distinguishes will and love, adding however that they concur. *Concurrent igitur voluntas et caritas*.[4] They concur in such a way that together they 'cause an act of love which is more perfect than will or even love could be on their own'. Is it possible that when he says this Scotus is thinking of the distinction he makes (and is accepted by Hopkins)[5] between affective will, which is drawn or attracted (magnetised, *aimanté*, *aimé*, loved), and elective will or what, on analogy with the 'agent intellect', we could call the 'agent will'? He subdivides the affective will into the *affectio iustitiae* of morality and the *affectio commodi*, which is the natural pull of one's desire for happiness and advantage.

However, at the beginning of a passage in which he distinguishes various meanings of 'natural' (as his compatriot David Hume will do in a famous footnote of the third appendix of *An Enquiry Concerning the Principles of Morals*) Scotus writes:

> the natural will is not really will at all, nor is natural volition true volition, for the term 'natural' effectively cancels or negates the sense of both 'will' and 'volition'. Nothing remains but the relationship a power has to its proper perfection.[6]

Its proper perfection is the good towards which it is naturally inclined. This is a passive tendency of power that at the same time 'tends freely and actively to elicit an act. Thus there is a twofold tendency in the one power, one active, the other passive'.[7] Note, by the way, that this is a duplicity of active and passive power, not the duplicity of active and passive voice that Locke does not distinguish adequately from it when he writes, in the words cited in our chapter on Peirce: 'Fire has a power to melt gold, i.e. to destroy the consistency of its insensible parts, and consequently its hardness, and make it fluid; and gold has a power to be melted . . .'

According to Scotus this duplicity of active and passive power (which overlaps the duplicity of willing and wanting) is crowned by a triplicity of the active power that is properly free. This freedom is exhibited in the possibility of an intermediate state of will that is neither willing-that (*velle*) nor willing-that-not (*nolle*), but choosing not to choose (*non velle*).[8] This third capacity to suspend judgement is exercised (actively exerted and passively provoked) for instance in the de-activating and de-willing of willed ignorance analysed in Chapter 11. It is the essence of what Scotus counts to be the rationality and the freedom of will that is compatible with natural necessity. Not willing is the self-restraint that is possible and may be rationally justifiable at the very moment when one either wills X or wills not-X. 'Hereby, I may tell you', as Hopkins tells Bridges in his letter of 4 January 1883 from Stonyhurst, 'hangs a very profound question treated by Duns Scotus, who shows that freedom is compatible with necessity.'

This suspension is also the essence of what we intend by 'attention', conceiving this following Augustine as a response to an explicit or implicit call to listen, to wait (*attendre*) and to wait upon, following Ignatius as *servire, attendere, contemplari*, following Hopkins as advertence, being ware, being aware, heed, regard, following Baker as observant observing, for instance the vigilant watching of the peregrine falcon, following Hopkins as one morning catching sight of, inscaping, The Windhover who is simultaneously for him the emphatically definite Word. This suspension thus conceived ranges beyond epistemically representative categorial or transcendental consciousness to ethico-religious reverence in the presence of God, if there be any, and therefore in the presence or absence or presence as absence of any existent what-or-whomsoever that can be in God's presence or absence.[9]

By what or by whom is this calling to attention made? By the being on whom we wait or by an advocate speaking on behalf of that being, an advocate who is the individuated self speaking anywhere and anywhen, for instance here and now, on behalf of something like the medially vocative activation of passivity that Heidegger calls letting-be (*Seinlassen*) and that we are calling attention understood as a willing not to will.

To will not to will is to make an intervention that liberates the will from a condition in which it is no more than one link in a chain of causes and turns it towards a condition in which it is free to effect its own change and to will even the suspension of its own will. It liberates us from the Aristotelo-Thomist necessitarianism of a causality of will moved only from outside.[10] Aristotle and Aquinas notwithstanding, attention is an 'indifference' that enables a science of the singular in which contingency is the power of a self-moving will to suspend both willing X and willing not-X.

This indifference is not lack of concern. On the contrary. It is a concern so profound as to merit the name love and this name's unadulteration, as in the moment of being struck by the marvel of pure existence in which, as Dennis Potter says, 'Things are both more trivial than they ever were, and more important than they ever were, and the difference between the trivial and the important doesn't seem to matter.'[11] Not sentimental love, not erotic love, not love concupiscent. Rather love ordered and ordained by justice to the singular: love that allows a communicability not only of common natures or universals, but of individual agents-cum-patients in a medially vocative chiasm of observation with observance and of intentionality with attentionality in which observation's proneness to become prying curiosity and intentionality's inclination towards authoritarianism are reversed by the power of the impower of supererogatory service without servitude.

'Reversed' (*à rebours*) is the expression that Levinas uses provisionally of the conversion of the Cartesian 'I' into the accused 'me' of responsible response. The word is used provisionally in the present context because, beyond a mere change of direction of intentionality, it looks and listens forward to the education of the power of intentionality's will by the impower of the will not to will. Hence the method of what in the last chapter was called educated ignorance is most educative and the exercise of will it performs is most respectful, most generous and least mean when methodology is also a *via amoris* for which any appeal made to the method of educated ignorance is an appeal to the experimental imagination. Only then is the beloved 'lovely' in the full sense of the word which, with the help especially of Scotus and Hopkins (and despite difficulties with the latter's iteration of the word 'beautiful'), this book has been trying to spell out.

The shudder-quotes in which we have just written the word 'reversed' are a warning to us not to forget another explanation attempted in this book and broached already in its first chapter, the explanation why the conjunction of intentionality and attentionality just proclaimed is neither a synthesis nor a reciprocal opposition.

The conjunction of intentionality and attentionality is not a reciprocal opposition or antithesis. Intending or meaning and the initial phase of patient attending are both performed or disposed to perform centri-fugally directed acts of pointing. Nevertheless, with the increase of intensity of attention there is an increase in the vulnerability of 'the world within' to the chance of finding not only the affect of self-taste but also the affect of aesthetic 'Apollonian' beauty transcended from 'the world without'. It is surprised, that is to say 'taken over' and 'overtaken' (*sur-pris*) by the 'Dionysian' aesthethical sublime that is marked in my misspelling of 'imadgination' with a d. Affect as the aesthesis of sensory impression is flooded by affect as aesthethical superimpression that strikes us either as hyperbolic goodness or as hyperbolic and ultra-transcendental threat or as the disjunction or conjunction of these.

The conjunction of intentionality and attentionality is not a synthesis. It is not a synthesis because its duality is not the dialectical duality of objects or objectives of consciousness. Intentionality understood as the of-ness of consciousness of objects or objectives, for instance of ideas, concepts or propositions, can be an exercise of will, for example when it is the affirmation of a belief. But it is not bound to be an exercise of will. Attention is arguably not this when, for example, it is attention to a feeling or sensation that 'grabs' our attention willy-nilly, *velle-nolle*. But Scotus, we have seen, followed by Hopkins, emphasises the importance of a third possibility, *non-velle*. This possibility can also be an option in the strict sense of being an exercise of will not to adopt either of the two original alternatives, *velle* and *nolle*. That is to say, this possibility can be an exercise of the will not to will. This is the possibility that distinguishes attention from intention. It is what puts attentionality at a different, ultra-categorial and ultra-transcendental level from intentionality, whether the latter be interpreted as the phenomenological of-ness of consciousness (the noetic-noematic hyphenation) or as the purposefulness of a deed that Hopkins calls 'forepitch'.[12] It is a meta-willing that transcends first-order willing, modifies it adverbially, postponing it in order to avoid a precipitateness that would lead to a failure to do justice to all the facts and things and persons liable to be affected by one's judgement. One's judgement in the sense of one's decision and intended deed is subjected in attention to one's judgement as sense for justice moved by love.

It should not be overlooked that judgement in this second sense of skill or wisdom – or indeed of discriminative common sensibility – calls to be engaged not only in deciding to wait (*attendre*) in order to avoid doing avoidable injustice. It calls to be engaged also lest avoidable injustice be done by waiting too long. Too soon or too late, judgement in this sense is a sense of timing.

Attentionality is convivial ethicality, in a generously ethical interpretation of this latter noun. It therefore crosses and hybridises the difference between the aesthetic and the ethical in the narrow interpretations of these terms in which they are opposed, and between the scientific if-then and the poetic as-if.[13] It thereby crosses the difference between aesthetically mimetic representation and poietic representation understood as celebration or hymn-singing, if not necessarily Him-singing, though not necessarily not.

What we have just been saying about the togetherness of intention and attention does not eliminate the distance between ostensively indicated and grammatically indicative *haecceitas* on the one hand and, on the other hand, the imperative Look! of *ecceitas* on which our reading of Hopkins' reading of Scotus has turned. Look! and See! and Hear! and Feel! are imperative variations on their respective verbal infinitives, to look, to hear and to feel. So they carry over into *ecceitas* the initial ostensively directive function of the intentionality of *haecceitas* taken as thisness. However, this carrying over is in service to a looking or feeling or sensation or affect or affection that are among what Hopkins finds when he says 'I find myself . . . ' This service is the observance of observation. It is the poet's – and the scientist's – priestliness. Without being subservience, this service is what German calls *Aufgabe*, 'vocation', the self's being called to give up (*auf-geben*) the claim to primacy both of its passivity and of its active intentionality in favour of the recipience of attention.

That is to say, the importation of intention into attention does not preclude the acquisition of a disposition to allow the intentness of intention itself to be informed by attentive regard understood as an enlargement of responsivity. This chiasmic interplay between intention and attention corresponds to the will not to will. It takes place across an ever narrowing gap closed only by death. This gap is a shortcoming in the degree of the, let us say, instress or pitch of our practical wisdom. The shortcomingness of this shortcoming can be overcome by the education of the will not to will. Could there be a more promising medium in which to conduct and characterise this education of the chiasm of intentive attention and attentive intention than what has been called in this book 'something like the middle voice', the voice of what has been called in this book the voice of address?

Address is what in his Comments on Loyola Hopkins calls the saying Yes, the Amen of, to speak barbarously, the 'doing-agree'.[14] If the doing that Hopkins finds in the notion of being as explained by Scotus is a changing or desiring or willing to change pitch, the doing-being that is the performance of an act of speech like the making of a poem will be a continual quest to rise beyond itself or a finding itself overcome by the benignly or unbenignly sublime: a *quaestio* that is older than any question answerable by the giving of information, at least as old as the quest Augustine says he has become to himself when he confesses *quaestio mihi factus sum*.[15]

The poem and the poet find themselves overcome by the world and the word, the world to which the word allows them to say 'yes, so be it', the world of which the sheer existence of the things in it is a prima facie ground for saying that word. Attentively sent or heard, or conveyed in an other than auditory medium, say vision or silence or dance, the word of address is a doing-agree to the extent that the sender and recipient share an understanding of at least a minimal lexicon and grammar. Via allusion to this, hence to the he, the she, the it, the we and the they of common naturality as distinguished from the I and the you of the haecceitico-ecceitic singularity of address, there arises the chance of gaining a foothold not only in landscapes and wordscapes of territories 'out there' but also in the scapes, inscapes and outscapes of which the foreignness is interior to where 'I find myself . . .', if I may borrow those words of avowal from Hopkins for a penultimate time. Thus Hopkins was already preparing the soil in which the seed of Scotist *distinctio formalis* would fall when the author of the essay on the Poem of Parmenides found himself in 'doing-agreement' with the author of the Poem to the extent of feeling that 'nothing is so pregnant and straightforward to the truth as simple *yes* and *is*'.[16]

There is more than one element by the addition of which this simplicity of affirmation may become a complicity. Let us remind ourselves here of just three such elements mentioned in the foregoing chapters. There are (1) the if-thenly element of abstractive and abductive generality given pride of place in Peirce's conception of natural science, (2) the element of individuality that figures in Hopkins' conception of the poem as a production of praise of the things of this and other as-ifly imaginable worlds, and (3) the hovering between the generality of science and the singularity of song exemplified by the great text of John Alec Baker, whether or not that singularity is a trace of the will of a Creator, as John Duns Scotus and Gerard Manley Hopkins believe it is. Whether it is this or is not, by distinguishing the numerical plurality of logical universality from the less than numerical unity of the common nature Scotus provides Hopkins with a metaphysical footing for the practice of an aesthethical rewording of the world in which at least momentarily the singularity of the irreplaceable inscapes of uniquely individual things is saved from degradation to the mere particularity of replaceable instances of abstracted or intuited universals.

However, if Scotus is in this way Hopkins' tutor, Hopkins is in turn tutor to Scotus' ghost. He is that when by ingenious design or ingenuous accident he drops the aitch from the word '*haecceitas*' that Scotus uses now and then of the ultimate and intimate cause or reason of individuality. When, *subito* and *subtilissime*, Hopkins does that he opens our eyes and alerts our ears to the ethicality of the transcendentally good, to the aestheticality of the transcendentally beautiful, and, moreover, to the aesthethicality (*sic*) of the trans-transcendentally affective sublime. This is better, more good, than the divine grace he grades as the 'better beauty'. It is better than that and more highly pitched because although its trans-transcendentality does not exclude the possibility of divine grace it allows too the possibility of the undivine and unreligioned but adogmatically religious love and justice of the vocation to will not to will in which unless he loses himself not even Hopkins can truthfully say 'I find myself'. The rule of substitution that licenses the equation of God with Love is a rule of substitution in more senses than one. It calls not only for a willingness to sacrifice one's selfwill for the sake (*Sache*) of the beloved. It calls also for the transcendence of divine grace by the immanence of a religious but not necessarily religioned attentivity of a willing not to will moved by the sheer existence of an individual or individuals other than oneself.

In his construction of an argument for a certain radical immanence

Categories and Transcendentals Transcended

Gilles Deleuze, although another philosopher under the spell of what Scotus says about *haecceitas*, is constrained nevertheless to treat Scotus as only a stepping stone to Spinoza in the development of that argument. That is because Spinoza's argument puts weight on attributes whereas Scotus believes that the weight which attributes can bear may be carried by properties, in particular the *propria* or intrinsic modes of the disjunction finite-infinite which he ranks among the Transcendentals.[17] Scotus holds that this disjunction opens a path to the transcendence of the finite by the infinite.

> In the disjunctive attributes . . . while the entire disjunction cannot be demonstrated from being, nevertheless as a universal rule by positing the less noble extreme of some being we can conclude that the more noble extreme is realised in some other being.[18]

The chances of Scotus' opening a path from transcendence to immanence via *haecceitas* or *ecceitas* would have been improved if he had spelled out more explicitly the difference between *ens* meaning entitivity and *ens* meaning and referring to an existent entity. Doing that would have required him to be more careful than some of his predecessors and contemporaries were to distinguish primary from secondary substance, more careful than perhaps he himself was in his dismissal of the materialist alternative to the haecceitic account of individuality preferred by him.[19]

The reference made in these last paragraphs of this last chapter to adogmatically religious love is not inconsistent with what may sound like a reference made here to a text of a historical dogmatic religion, namely Luke 9: 24, which says, 'For whosoever will save his life shall lose it: but whosoever will lose his life for my sake, the same shall save it.' Sake. That is to say, as Hopkins would have us say, *Sache*, that by which I am abroad from myself and perhaps therefore, as Goethe's Faust would have us say, *tremens, schaudernd*, ashudder.

Afterword

The gospel of the book to which an afterword is now in process of being appended here has been that the good spell may be but does not have to be a God's spell. The religious in defence of which this news of necessary contingency speaks may be illuminated by this or that religion, so it does not preach the necessity of atheism or secularism. Nor however is it a derivative of a religion or a deduction from a Book. It is an exercise in *Seinlassen*, in letting being be in such a manner that justice is done at the same time to beings by following a path opened up by the author of a *Treatise on Duns Scotus' Theory of Categories and Signification*.[1] More specifically, it is an exercise aimed at removing what to some potential readers of Scotus and Hopkins might present itself as a stumbling block to their becoming actual readers of the singular philosophical and poetical entities created by these two writers, to wit the theological presuppositions of their writings.

These theological presuppositions and how they draw the Scottish Franciscan and the English Jesuit together are studied meticulously by Christopher Devlin SJ in his edition of Hopkins' *Sermons and Devotional Writings*. However, he scrupulously and explicitly eschews what he deems to be more purely or technically philosophical discussion. What I eschew is the more purely or technically theological discussion. I do this out of an acute awareness of my incompetence in that domain. Yet I do not do it without acknowledgement of an obligation to attempt to render that incompetence less crass. My discourse has been for the most part philosophical. But in adopting that discourse and in imitation of the carefulness with which Scotus considers the relation of the metaphysical to the theological in the prologue to the *Questions on the Metaphysics of Aristotle* and in *Reportatio* I A210[2] I have tried to avoid complacency over the question how the languages of philosophy, theology and poetry adapt to or unravel one another when one of them becomes a source of metaphors for one or more of the others.

'Metaphor' is a metaphor for 'image', and 'image' is an image for 'metaphor'. This stands for that as a likeness or this is identified with that. The one represents the other aesthetico-speculatively or ethically or aesthethically, therefore implicating the will or the will not to will of self-command. This is a self-command that for Scotus and Hopkins wills to be one with the command of God and in (the image of) Christ. For according to them and to Ephesians 2:10, 'We are his design; God has created us in Christ Jesus . . .' 'Design' is the translation Devlin prefers for the Greek text's *poiēma*. He thereby induces us to recognise that when Hopkins equates inscape with design inscape inherits the idea of directedness to an end. Hence when Hopkins offers also 'pattern' as an equivalent the sense of pattern as exemplar or paradigm is in play. No wonder then that he asks us to think of being as doing. This is another way of saying, as the title of our second chapter says, that inscape is stressed. And this in turn is a way of saying that although for Hopkins inscapes are the subject matter of his poetry of the natural 'world without', human willing is mixed in with the labour of the production of the poem by the makar, its *poiēma*; as in 'The Poem of Parmenides'; as in the work of our willing in the world within and at the thresholds between the within and the without; as between human nature and divine nature of which we recall Hopkins saying: 'It is as if a man said: That is Christ playing at me and me playing at Christ, only that it is no play but truth; That is Christ *being me* and me being Christ' (GMH's emphasis).[3] It is as if a man said play *as if* it were truth (JL's emphasis), wordplay, *Wortspiel*, taken seriously, as if to say 'Take my word for it', as if (to spell it out as what we have chosen to call an 'emphatically definite description') it were The Word's play, Gospel. For the metaphor, the image and the analogy are works of imagination through which, as illustrated in the works of Hopkins and Baker, the 'as if' is capable of application to the 'if-then' of factuality and fate or historical destiny. But this application is not compelled. The imagination may be the mediator between commonality and singularity, or between universality and particularity as Kant maintains in his comments on schematism, but imagination is neutral with respect to factual truth. It leaves unsettled the choice between fiction and fact. It operates according to the form that the factual shares with the fictive, a likeness without which we could not be deceived or practice the pretence that, we have just seen, Hopkins describes as playing-at. It is the patient agency or agent patiency at work in the creating of (a) creation.

We have said that there are some grounds for saying that for Scotus and Hopkins Beauty is a Cinderella Transcendental despite references to it in their works.[4] There are some grounds for saying also that despite disagreements with Thomists in the writings of Scotus and in medieval writings more generally over the role of *phantasia* and *imaginatio*, imagination remains for all of these authors a Cinderella dimension of mentality. She does not get to go to the ball until she is shown the way by the Kant of the first edition of the first Critique,[5] by Schelling, by Coleridge, by Heidegger as the author of *Kant and the Problem of Metaphysics*, and by an author introduced at the beginning of our second chapter, Hopkins' mentor John Ruskin, who writes of the 'penetrating possession-taking faculty of Imagination . . . the highest intellectual power of man'.[6] Such high praise as is lavished by Ruskin here would not have been unexpected had we found it expressed on pages written by Scotus, for to elevate imagination is to elevate the importance of freedom of will. The will is the power of mind to which Scotus offers the palm because it is the power to dispossess oneself of power. My willing not to will, which is the regard attention pays to intention, is my preparedness to free up a way for what is other than myself to surprise me, to come at me out of the blue. It is what liberates me to 'blue sky' thinking and Mallarmé's *azur*. Willing not to will is a disponible waiting for the coming of one knows not what: what may turn out to be unsolicited thoughts the thinking *of* which is both 'subjectively' and 'objectively' genitive. At once left-brained and right-brained, both *yin* and *yang*, the nouns and pronouns of the language in which those thoughts are expressed and addressed are ambiguously gendered and the verbs middle-voiced or deponent (grammatically passive but semantically active). Together they postpone indefinitely judgement, prejudgement, prejudice and choice, for instance the choice between a hypothesis affirmed or denied in the light of empirical evidence and a supposition entertained, 'played at', between 'myth' as implying falsity and myth minus that implication.

It is because a religion may be a mythology construed according to this second sense of the word 'myth' that we can legitimately cease to perceive the religion of Scotus and Hopkins as an insurmountable barrier to our ability to read their works or to our regarding our doing so as rewarding. The religious, we have said, we hope not dogmatically, is not bound either to include or to exclude any specific historical religion. This is why the unravelling of their writings may be allowed to give way now at the end of our study to what, at the end of its second epigraph, Hopkins calls peace, meaning the peace to which he says his spirit was swayed by the spell of John Duns Scotus.

Except that, on the evidence of Hopkins' Dublin years at least, that peace was destined to be intermittent, disturbed by anxiety lest dogmatism or complacency prevail over attentiveness or love, fated to be stressed by (NB) the specifically *philosophical* dilemma alluded to in the words adopted as this book's other epigraph, the philosophical dilemma of which Hopkins himself says that it will not let him rest. By this he means perhaps, in the spirit of his endorsement of Scotus' exegesis of human being as a doing of free will, that (to speak barbarously, in the language of the stranger that twists our tongue) he will will not to let it let him. He will will not to let it let him not necessarily out of what he might have called divine discontent, but out of a discontent that would be better described or left undescribed by the word 'sublime'. For the adventure of a sublimity that is bindingly religious without being bound to be a religion promises or threatens more than does the advent of a divinity. Whether or not this promise is kept or this threat realised will always remain to be learned if the attention demanded by the love that waits to learn this is just, that is to say empty of prejudice and creatively 'decreative'.

I use this last word in the sense approximating that given it by Simone Weil when she writes that to decreate is 'to make something created pass into the uncreated',[7] and 'We participate in the creation of the world by decreating ourselves.'[8] She restricts the word 'decreative' to a love that is the love of God, hence, given that God is love, to a God that loves himself. 'In so far as I become nothing, God loves himself through me.'[9] Common ground between her and my understanding of the decreativity of the creature's love is that this love practises an emptying of egoity, though not to the point that it is so devoid of ego that there is no ego to surrender for love's sake and no possibility of willing not to will. However, her understanding of decreative love is God-centred. Mine is decentred. I understand the decreativity of love as what Hopkins was touching on but just failing to touch when he wrote of a 'better beauty'. My word for that is 'sublimity', meaning the sublimity of a *kenōsis* that promises or (remembering Goethe's words about shuddering humanity quoted in Chapter 1 and not forgetting that a promise can also be a threat) promises or 'promises' more than God's most, even if this most is that of the superlativity of the perfection presumed to be non-self-contradictory in Scotus' 'colouring' of Anselm's ontological argument and supplied to the concept of God by the concept of God's existence.

Unless God, exceeding theoretical conceptuality and its law of logical non-contradiction, stands, as theologians tell us He does, in a hyperlogical but formally distinct relationship with Love, and Love, like Being according to Hopkins and Scotus, is practice: the practice of willing not to will, of power over power, and of the astonished wonder in which begin, philosophers including The Philosopher tell us, the theoretico-practical love of wisdom, that is to say philosophy itself, and, formally distinct from philosophy, the ethical, aesthethical and religious or 'religious'

Afterword

practico-theoretical wisdom of love for which Hopkins might have created the barbarous neologism 'sophophily'.

Not a barbarous neologism but a familiar term in Simone Weil's vocabulary is the word 'attention'. Should she have paid more attention to the implications of the diagnosis attributed to Saint Thomas, the Angelic Doctor, that the sin of Lucifer and his fellow fallen angels was an attention deficit disorder?[10] Should we? For the word 'attention' has also become familiar in the vocabulary invoked in this book. It will have become too familiar unless it maintains its chiasmic and middle-voiced hence receptively active and actively receptive but non-synthetic proto-relationship with 'intention'. The expansion of Simone Weil's conception of decreative love sketched in the paragraphs immediately preceding this one is an expansion of her in my opinion too limited conception of attention.[11] That conception is too limited, I opine, in several respects: it is too inattentive to what is other than God; it is too inhospitable to the strangeness that exceeds essence in Hopkins' transformation of formal essence into deformal and sometimes deformed, ugly or 'ugly' inscape; it is blind to his respelling of *haecceitas* as *ecceitas*; it is deaf to the Scotist metaphysics of common naturality cruxed with individuality; it pays no heed to the consequences of interpreting that metaphysics in the light of a reading of Parmenides' hyphenation of being and thinking as a 'simple yes' that affirms an interiority of the verb to the noun. These limitations are all symptoms of a deficiency of attention to the unlimitation of the unpossible possibility of an exteriority that sends a shudder through traditional logics and grammars of class inclusion, predication, categoriality and transcendentality. They are symptoms of inattention to the revelation of the existence of the existent in its or Its thisness or thatness come what or who gratuitously may.

Notes

CHAPTER 1

1. Claude Colleer Abbott (ed.), *The Letters of Gerard Manley Hopkins to Robert Bridges* (London: Oxford University Press, 1955), p. 209.
2. Karl Abel, 'The Antithetical Sense of Primal Words', reviewed in James Strachey (ed.), *Standard Edition of the Complete Psychological Works of Sigmund Freud* (London: Hogarth Press, 1955), pp. 218ff. See also John Llewelyn, *Derrida on the Threshold of Sense* (London: Macmillan, 1986), pp. 85ff.
3. In Chapter 6 and Chapter 11.
4. Ludwig Wittgenstein, *Philosophical Investigations*, trans. G. E. M. Anscombe (Oxford: Blackwell, 1953), p. 47.
5. Émile Benveniste, *Problèmes de linguistique générale* (Paris: Gallimard, 1966), vol. I, p. 172. Llewelyn, *Derrida on the Threshold of Sense*, pp. 90–4.
6. Johann Wolfgang von Goethe, *Faust* Part II, in Karl Heinemann (ed.), *Goethes Werke*, 30 vols (Leipzig and Vienna: Bibliographisches Institut, 1900–8), vol. 5, line 6272.
7. See John Llewelyn, *Margins of Religion: Between Kierkegaard and Derrida* (Bloomington: Indiana University Press, 2009), *The Rigor of a Certain Inhumanity: Toward a Wider Suffrage* (Bloomington: Indiana University Press, 2012).
8. See Chapter 6.

CHAPTER 2

1. Humphry House (ed.), *The Note-Books and Papers of Gerard Manley Hopkins* (London: Oxford University Press, 1937), pp. 153–4.
2. Ibid. p. 101. Norman H. MacKenzie, *A Reader's Guide to Gerard Manley*

Hopkins (London: Thames and Hudson, 1981), p. 233. Humphry House (ed.), *The Journals and Papers of Gerard Manley Hopkins* (London: Oxford University Press, 1959), pp. 175, 204–5.
3. *The Letters of Gerard Manley Hopkins to Robert Bridges*, p. 83.
4. See Walter J. Ong SJ, 'Hopkins' Sprung Rhythm and the Life of English Poetry', in Norman Weyand SJ (ed.), *Immortal Diamond: Studies in Gerard Manley Hopkins* (London: Sheed and Ward, 1949), p. 96.
5. *The Letters of Gerard Manley Hopkins to Robert Bridges*, p. 162.
6. William Barnes, *Early England and the Saxon-English; with some notes on the father-stock of the Saxon-English, the Frisians* (London: John Russell Smith, 1869).
7. In a letter to Bridges dated 26 September 1882, Hopkins wrote: 'I did in my last week at Roehampton write 16 pages of a rough draft of a commentary on St Ignatius' Spiritual Exercises. This work would interest none but a Jesuit, but to me it is interesting enough and, as you see, it is very professional.' I hope that my commentary on his commentary demonstrates that Hopkins underestimated the range of the audience for whom that latter document would be of interest. (*The Letters of Gerard Manley Hopkins to Robert Bridges*, p. 150.)
8. Étienne Gilson, *L'être et l'essence* (Paris: Vrin, 1949), pp. 13–15.
9. *The Note-Books and Papers of Gerard Manley Hopkins*, p. 171.
10. Ibid. pp. 216–17.
11. Ibid. p. 114.
12. Ibid, p. 144.
13. See below, Chapter 5, and Scotus, *Ordinatio* 1, d. 3, p. 1, qq. 1–2, n. 26–n. 45. Depending on the question of the authenticity of certain commentaries on Aristotle, scholars have been divided on whether Scotus' own metaphysical doctrine developed from analogism to univocalism. See Cyril L. Shircel, OFM, *The Univocity of the Concept of Being in the Philosophy of John Duns Scotus* (Washington, DC: The Catholic University of America, 1942). See also essays gathered under the heading 'Being and Univocity' in Ludger Honnefelder, Rega Wood and Mechthild Dreyer (eds), *John Duns Scotus: Metaphysics and Ethics* (Leiden: Brill, 1996) and Peter King, 'Scotus on Metaphysics', in Thomas Williams (ed.), *The Cambridge Companion to Duns Scotus* (Cambridge: Cambridge University Press, 2002), pp. 18–21.
14. *The Note-Books and Papers of Gerard Manley Hopkins*, p. 337.
15. Ibid. p. 140.
16. Ibid. p. 145.
17. Kate Kellaway, *The Guardian*, 19 January 2013, in a review of Kathleen Jamie's volume of poems titled *The Overhaul* (London: Picador, 2012).
18. Paul Vincent Spade, trans., *Five Texts on the Mediaeval Problem of Universals: Porphyry, Boethius, Abelard, Duns Scotus, Ockham* (Indianapolis: Hackett, 1994), pp. 65–6.
19. Philologists, that is to say word lovers, will have noticed that the pronunciation of the very word 'wander' currently wanders between rhyming and

not rhyming with English 'fonder' and that the pronunciation of the word 'wonder' wanders between rhyming and not rhyming with 'thunder'. As far as I have noticed, the first syllable of 'wondrous' (see below) still rhymes with 'fun'. (Watch this space.)
20. An interview with Melvyn Bragg broadcast by BBC Channel 4 on 5 April 1994, two months before Potter died.
21. Wittgenstein, *Philosophical Investigations*, p. 66.
22. From 'The Starlight Night', the first line of which already bids us 'Look at the stars! look, look up at the skies!'
23. *The Note-Books and Papers of Gerard Manley Hopkins*, p. 309.
24. Martin Heidegger, *Wegmarken, Gesamtausgabe* 9, ed. Friedrich Wilhelm von Hermann (Frankfurt am Main: Klostermann, 1976), p. 306. Martin Heidegger, 'Postscript to *What is Metaphysics?*', in William McNeill (ed.), *Pathmarks* (Cambridge: Cambridge University Press, 1998), p. 233.
25. Christopher Devlin SJ (ed.), *The Sermons and Devotional Writings of Gerard Manley Hopkins* (London: Oxford University Press, 1959), p. 109.
26. John Duns Scotus, *Philosophical Writings: A Selection*, trans. Allan B. Wolter (Indianapolis: Bobbs-Merrill, 1978), pp. 3–13.

CHAPTER 3
1. *The Note-Books and Papers of Gerard Manley Hopkins*, p. 362.
2. Ibid. p. 98.
3. Ibid. pp. 98–9.
4. J. Hillis Miller, 'The Univocal Chiming', in Geoffrey H. Hartman (ed.), *Hopkins: A Collection of Critical Essays* (Englewood Cliffs: Prentice-Hall, 1966).
5. *The Note-Books and Papers of Gerard Manley Hopkins*, p. 75.
6. Ibid. p. 99.
7. Ibid. p. 100.
8. Incidentally, a typographical dash is called in Danish a *tankestreg*, a think-stroke.
9. *The Note-Books and Papers of Gerard Manley Hopkins*, p. 100.
10. See below, Chapter 5 and Chapter 12.
11. *The Note-Books and Papers of Gerard Manley Hopkins*, p. 322.
12. House, *The Journals and Papers of Gerard Manley Hopkins*, p. 192. The importance for my argument in this book and elsewhere of the distinction between my catching sight of and my eye being caught was brought home to me by a passing remark made by Rowan Williams in responding to queries following one of the Gifford Lectures he delivered at Edinburgh in 2013. Rowan Williams, *The Edge of Words* (London: Bloomsbury, 2014).
13. Contrast with Muybridge's freezing Rudolf Steiner's unfreezing of figures in his theory of how geometry should be taught, reminding us of Kant's founding geometry on the procedure of a schematism in imagination that applies principles for generating diagrams.
14. See below, Chapter 6.

15. Martin Heidegger, 'Schöpferische Landschaft: Warum bleiben wir in der Provinz?' in Hermann Heidegger (ed.), *Denkerfahrungen* (Frankfurt am Main: Klostermann, 1983), p. 9. If the adverb *eigentlich* ('authentic') is taken as an opposite of *uneigentlich* in Heidegger's special sense of the word, his remark verges on tautology. In that sense the *betrachten eigentlich* of a landscape is by definition disallowed by the verb. Gazing at views is what tourists do, and tourism is an inauthentic way of passing time, a pastime. 'Authentic gawking' is an oxymoron.
16. *The Note-Books and Papers of Gerard Manley Hopkins*, p. 322.
17. Ibid.
18. Alexander P. D. Mourelatos, *The Route of Parmenides*, revised and expanded edn (Las Vegas, Zürich, Athens: Parmenides Publishing, 2008), p. 48.
19. *The Note-Books and Papers of Gerard Manley Hopkins*, pp. 100–1.
20. Ibid. p. 338.
21. See above, Chapter 1.
22. *The Note-Books and Papers of Gerard Manley Hopkins*, p. 323.
23. Ibid. p. 328.

CHAPTER 4

1. W. H. Gardner (ed.), *Gerard Manley Hopkins: Poems and Prose* (London: Penguin Books, 1963), p. 169.
2. *The Letters of Gerard Manley Hopkins to Robert Bridges*, pp. 30–1.
3. As we shall find reason to say in the Afterword.
4. *The Note-Books and Papers of Gerard Manley Hopkins*, pp. 309–10.
5. The continuation and context of this text will be examined in Chapter 10.
6. Martin Heidegger, *Frühe Schriften*, Gesamtausgabe 1, ed. Friedrich-Wilhelm von Hermann (Frankfurt am Main: Klostermann, 1978), p. 258/195. Martin Heidegger, *Traité des catégories et de la signification chez Duns Scotus*, trans. Florent Gaboriau (Paris: Gallimard, 1970), p. 78.
7. Oleg Bychkov has reminded me that the letter '*h*' was commonly omitted in medieval manuscripts because it was no longer pronounced. (A *quid pro quo* in anticipation of its commonly not being omitted from the letter's spoken name?)
8. F. P. Ramsey, 'General Propositions and Causality', in R. B. Braithwaite (ed.), *F. P. Ramsey: The Foundations of Mathematics* (London: Routledge and Kegan Paul, 1931), p. 238.
9. *The Note-Books and Papers of Gerard Manley Hopkins*, p. 328.
10. Ibid. pp. 98–9.
11. Scotus, *Ordinatio* lib. II. d. 3, p. 1. q. 6, 172.
12. Ibid. qq. 1–6.
13. Wittgenstein, *Philosophical Investigations*, 38.
14. Ibid. p. 276.
15. See below, Chapter 7.
16. *The Note-Books and Papers of Gerard Manley Hopkins*, p. 249.

17. John Llewelyn, *Departing from Logic: Returning to Wales* (Talybont, Ceredigion: Y Lolfa, 2012).
18. See below, Chapter 8.
19. *The Note-Books and Papers of Gerard Manley Hopkins*, p. 310.
20. Ibid. p. 98.
21. See below, Chapter 9.

CHAPTER 5

1. Heidegger, *Frühe Schriften*, p. 144/202, *Traité*, p. 32.
2. Frederick Copleston, SJ, *A History of Philosophy*, vol. 2, *Mediaeval Philosophy: Augustine to Scotus* (London: Burns Oates & Washbourne, 1959), p. 499.
3. John Austin, 'A Plea for Excuses', in *Philosophical Papers*, ed. J. O. Urmson and G. J. Warnock (Oxford: Oxford University Press, 1961), pp. 123–52.
4. Wittgenstein, *Philosophical Investigations*, 66.
5. Edward Thomas, *Letters to George Bottomley*, ed. R. George Thomas (London: Oxford University Press, 1968), letter of 7 February 1908 written at Minsmere. For this reference I am indebted again to Robert Macfarlane, who first brought my attention to Thomas' sentence in readings broadcast on BBC Radio 3 in Autumn 2009 (later repeated) in the series entitled The Essay. See Llewelyn, *The Rigor of a Certain Inhumanity*, pp. 212ff.
6. See above, Chapter 1.
7. *The Note-Books and Papers of Gerard Manley Hopkins*, p. 100.
8. Hereinafter he will usually be referred to as Scotus, as he is by Heidegger. The theory of categories on which Heidegger's commentary is based is due to Scotus, but the theory of signification is now attributed to the Scotist Thomas of Erfurt.
9. Heidegger, *Frühe Schriften*, pp. 410–11/552–3, *Traité*, p. 231.
10. John Duns Scotus, *Opus Oxoniense*, lib. II, d. III. q. I. (10).
11. Joseph Butler, *Fifteen Sermons Printed at the Rolls Chapel* (Cambridge: Hilliard and Brown, 1726), §39.
12. John Duns Scotus, *Quaest. super Met.*, lib. V. q. XII.
13. Ibid. lib. IV. q. I.
14. Alexander of Hales, *Summa Theologica* (Quaracchi: Saint Bonaventura University), I, n. 103; t. I. 162, cited by Allan B. Wolter, *The Transcendentals and their Function in the Metaphysics of Duns Scotus* (New York: Franciscan Institute of St Bonaventure, 1946), p. 100.
15. Martin Heidegger, 'Platons Lehre von der Wahrheit', in Friedrich Wilhelm von Hermann (ed.), Martin Heidegger, *Wegmarken, Gesamtausgabe* 9 (Frankfurt am Main: Klostermann, 1976); William McNeill (ed.), *Pathmarks* (Cambridge: Cambridge University Press, 1998).
16. John Grote, *Exploratio Philosophica*, Part I (Cambridge: Deighton Bell, 1865), Part II (Cambridge: Deighton Bell, 1900).
17. Heinrich Rickert, *Science and History: A Critique of Positivist Epistemology*, trans. Georg Reisman (New York: Van Nostrand, 1962), p. 154, n. 3. See also

Notes

Friedrich Hogemann, *Dimensionen des Logischen* (Frankfurt am Main: Peter Lang, 2013); *Dimensions of the Logical*, trans. John Llewelyn, forthcoming.
18. Heidegger, *Frühe Schriften*, p. 279/221, *Traité*, p. 107.
19. *The Note-Books and Papers of Gerard Manley Hopkins*, p. 100.
20. Ibid. p. 313.
21. Ibid. p. 312.

CHAPTER 6

1. *The Note-Books and Papers of Gerard Manley Hopkins*, pp. 148–9.
2. See Llewelyn, *Margins of Religion*, pp. 324–5.
3. The word 'term' was used of something non-verbal when it was applied to the 'successive sidings' of the inscape of the flag flower in the first of the group of three dated entries cited above from his journal.
4. Gottfried Wilhelm Leibniz, *Philosophical Papers and Letters*, second edn, ed. Leroy E. Loemker (Dordrecht: Reidel, 1969), p. 60, n. 23, p. 120, n. 17.
5. In Chapter 7.
6. *The Note-Books and Papers of Gerard Manley Hopkins*, pp. 80, 85, 89.
7. Scotus, *Opus Oxoniense*, lib. III. d. XX. q. I, p. 41a, §D. *Sermons and Devotional Writings of Gerard Manley Hopkins*, pp. 109, 297.
8. *Sermons and Devotional Writings of Gerard Manley Hopkins*, p. 351.
9. E. T. Cook and Alexander Wedderburn (eds), *The Works of John Ruskin*, 39 vols (London: George Allen, 1903–1912), vol. iv, p. 369.
10. Immanuel Kant, 'Concerning the ultimate ground of the differentiation of directions in space', in D. Walford and R. Meerboote (eds), *The Cambridge Edition of the Works of Immanuel Kant: Theoretical Philosophy, 1755–1770* (Cambridge: Cambridge University Press, 1992), pp. 365–72.
11. *Sermons and Devotional Writings of Gerard Manley Hopkins*, p. 195.
12. Unlike the familiar expression 'needs must', 'needs would' allows to man a freedom to choose or not to choose such worhip. It is another example of Hopkins' venturing into the realm of syntactico-semantic obscurity, one of the kind Dylan Thomas will frequently imitate. Both imitate Heraclitus, who was known as The Obscure. All three, in their endeavours to convey a sense of what it is for something to be in process of creation and to give it for the first time a name, a Word or a *Logos*, testify that they can best get this sense across in a language that retains traces of nonsense.
13. *The Note-Books and Papers of Gerard Manley Hopkins*, p. 332.
14. Ibid. pp. 317–18.
15. *Sermons and Devotional Writings of Gerard Manley Hopkins*, pp. 174–5.
16. Mary Beth Ingham and Mechthild Dreyer, *The Philosophical Vision of John Duns Scotus: An Introduction* (Washington, DC: The Catholic University of America Press, 2004), p. 175.
17. Scotus, *Ordinatio* lib. I, d. 17, n. 62. Allan B. Wolter. OFM (ed. and trans.), *Duns Scotus on the Will and Morality* (Washington, DC: The Catholic University of America Press, 1986), p. 207.

CHAPTER 7

1. J. A. Baker, *The Peregrine: The Hill of Summer & Diaries*, ed. John Fanshawe (London: HarperCollins, 2010, 2011), p. 30.
2. Baker, *The Peregrine*, p. 31.
3. Ibid.
4. Baker, *The Hill of Summer*, p. 260.
5. Ibid. p. 258.
6. Baker, *The Peregrine*, p. 58.
7. Baker, *The Hill of Summer*, p. 261.
8. Ibid. p. 254.
9. Ibid. p. 293.
10. Richard Dawkins, *The God Delusion* (London: Bantam, 2006).
11. Though if an example is an instantiation of a universal, of what other than an Exemplar can something unique be an example?
12. Baker, *The Hill of Summer*, p. 320.
13. Ibid. p. 264.
14. Ibid. pp. 212–13.
15. Baker, *The Peregrine*, p. 28.
16. Baker, *The Hill of Summer*, p. 301.
17. Ibid. p. 259.
18. Ibid. p. 216.
19. Ibid. p. 239.
20. James Gleick, *The Information: A History, A Theory, A Flood* (London: Fourth Estate, 2012).

CHAPTER 8

1. Charles Hartshorne, Paul Weiss et al. (eds), *Collected Papers of Charles Sanders Peirce* (Cambridge, MA: The Belknap Press of Harvard University Press, 1931–58), 5.400.
2. *The Note-Books and Papers of Gerard Manley Hopkins*, p. 309.
3. John Locke, *An Essay Concerning Human Understanding*, II.XXI.1.
4. Ibid. II.XXI.75.
5. Ibid. II.I.3.
6. Peirce, CP, 1.304, 1.25.
7. Peirce, CP, 1.357, 1.23.
8. Peirce, CP, 6.361.
9. Peirce, CP, 4.179, 427, 504. See Llewelyn, *The Rigor of a Certain Inhumanity*, pp. 60–4.
10. See Murray G. Murphey, *The Development of Peirce's Philosophy* (Cambridge, MA: Harvard University Press, 1961), pp. 313–14.
11. See John F. Boler, *Charles Sanders Peirce and Scholastic Realism: A Study of Peirce's Relation to John Duns Scotus* (Seattle: University of Washington Press, 1963), pp. 142, 149.

Notes

12. Peirce, CP, 5.436.
13. Peirce, CP, 1.368.
14. *The Letters of Gerard Manley Hopkins to Robert Bridges*, p. 83.
15. Peirce, CP, 1.369.
16. Immanuel Kant, *Kant's Critique of Practical Reason and Other Works on the Theory of Ethics*, trans. Thomas Kingsmill Abbott (London: Longmans, 1959), p. xiii.
17. Peirce, CP, 5.312.
18. John Duns Scotus, *Quaestiones subtilissimae super libros Metaphysicorum Aristotelis*, lib. 7. q. 18.
19. John Duns Scotus, *Questions on the Metaphysics of Aristotle*, 2 vols, trans. G. J. Etzkorn and A. B. Wolter (New York: St Bonaventure University, 1998), Book VII, Question Eighteen, para. 59.
20. Peirce, CP, 5.301.
21. Peirce, CP, 5.430.
22. Peirce, CP, 1.21.
23. See Boler, *Charles Sanders Peirce and Scholastic Realism*, p. 64.
24. For a treatment of this distinction see Jorge J. E. Gracia, 'Individuality and the Individuating Entity in Scotus' *Ordinatio*: An Ontological Characterization', in Ludger Honnefelder, Rega Wood and Mechthild Dreyer (eds), *John Duns Scotus: Metaphysics and Ethics* (Leiden: Brill, 1996), pp. 229–49.

CHAPTER 9

1. King, 'Scotus on Metaphysics', p. 60, n. 33. Andrew J. O'Brien, 'Duns Scotus' Teaching on the Distinction Between Essence and Existence', in *The New Scholasticism 38*, 61–77.
2. John Duns Scotus, *Commentaria Oxoniensia*, ed. P. M. F. Garcia OFM (Quaracchi, Florence: Ad Claras Aquas, 1914), lib. II. d. XVI. q. I. (10).
3. Scotus, *Reportatio Parisiensia*, lib. I. d. II, q. 3. *Opus Oxoniense*, lib. I. d. II. q. II. no. 32. Duns Scotus, *Philosophical Writings*, pp. 77ff. *Duns Scotus Metaphysician*, ed. and trans. William A. Frank and Allan B. Wolter (West Lafayette: Purdue University Press, 1995), pp. 65ff.
4. Llewelyn, *The Rigor of a Certain Inhumanity*.
5. David Hume, *A Treatise of Human Nature*, ed. L. A. Selby-Bigge (Oxford: Clarendon Press, 1888), I.II.VI, pp. 66–7.
6. Pierre Alféri, *Guillaume d'Ockham: le singulier* (Paris: Editions de Minuit, 1989), pp. 141ff. Emphases in the original.
7. See the pages referred to under 'schematism' in the index of John Llewelyn, *The HypoCritical Imagination: Between Kant and Levinas* (London and New York: Routledge, 2000).
8. Marilyn McCord Adams, *William Ockham* (Notre Dame: University of Notre Dame Press, 1987), vol. 1, pp. 47ff.
9. Jacques Derrida, *The Beast and the Sovereign, Vol. II*, ed. Michel Lisse, Marie-Louise Mallet and Ginette Michaud, trans. Geoffrey Bennington (Chicago:

The University of Chicago Press, 2011), p. xvi, n.8, p. 265, n.10. Jacques Derrida, 'Justices', in Barbara Cohen and Dragan Kujunžic (eds), *Provocations to Reading: J. Hillis Miller and the Democracy to Come* (New York: Fordham University Press, 2005).
10. In Chapter 4.
11. *The Note-Books and Papers of Gerard Manley Hopkins*, p. 328. Emphasis added.
12. Jacques Derrida, *Otobiographies: l'enseignement de Nietzsche et la politique du nom propre* (Paris: Galilée, 1984).
13. *The Note-Books and Papers of Gerard Manley Hopkins*, p. 171.
14. John Duns Scotus, *Commentaria Oxoniensia*, ed. P. M. F. Garcia OFM (Quaracchi, Florence: Ad Claras Aquas, 1914), lib. II. d. XVI. q. I. (10).
15. Thomas Reid, *Works*, Vol. I (Edinburgh: MacLachlan and Stewart, 1863), p. 434.
16. *The Note-Books and Papers of Gerard Manley Hopkins*, pp. 102, 314, 315.

CHAPTER 10

1. *The Note-Books and Papers of Gerard Manley Hopkins*, pp. 100–1.
2. Ibid. p. 328.
3. See above, Chapter 3. The Welsh particle *a* functions here somewhat as does the English relative pronoun 'who'.
4. D. M. Armstrong, *Nominalism and Realism: Universals and Scientific Realism I* (Cambridge: Cambridge University Press, 1978), p. 10.
5. *The Note-Books and Papers of Gerard Manley Hopkins*, p. 182.
6. Ibid. p. 198.
7. *The Spiritual Exercises of Saint Ignatius Loyola*, trans. W. H. Longridge (London: Robert Scott, 1919), p. 26.
8. Claude Colleer Abbott (ed.), *The Correspondence of Gerard Manley Hopkins and Richard Watson Dixon* (London: Oxford University Press, 1955), p. 88.
9. *The Note-Books and Papers of Gerard Manley Hopkins*, p. 174.

CHAPTER 11

1. See above, Chapter 4.
2. Llewelyn, *Margins of Religion*.
3. Nicolous Cusanus, *Of Learned Ignorance*, trans. Germain Heron (London: Routledge and Kegan Paul, 1954), p. 9.
4. See above, Chapter 5.
5. *Sermons and Devotional Writings of Gerard Manley Hopkins*, pp. 293 and 342. Devlin seems to give as the source of these Latin words John Duns Scotus, *Reportatio Parisiensia*, lib. II. d. XII. q. V. However, I have been unable to track these words down, though there are sentences at that reference that convey their gist.
6. Scotus, *Opus Oxoniense*, lib. I, d. II, qq. i and ii. Ockham, *Quaestiones in lib.*

Notes

I Physicorum, q. cxxxv, in *Ockham: Philosophical Writings*, ed. and trans. Philotheus Boehner, OFM (Edinburgh: Nelson, 1957), pp. 118–22.

CHAPTER 12

1. Hannah Arendt, *The Life of the Mind* (London, New York: Harcourt, 1978), p. 31.
2. Ibid. *Willing*, p. 136.
3. I write 'act or quasi-act' in order to avoid the infinite regress threatened by treating willing as an act like any other. In what way would it be unlike any other? How does willing relate to being willing? These are important questions, but not for the limited purpose that concerns us here.
4. Scotus, *Lectura* lib. I. d. XVII. q. 79.
5. *The Note-Books and Papers of Gerard Manley Hopkins*, pp. 325–9.
6. '... *voluntas naturalis non est voluntatis nec velle naturale est velle, sed naturalis distrahit ab utroque et nihil est nisi relatio consequens potentiam respectu propriae perfectionis.*' Scotus, *Ordinatio* lib. III. d. 17. *Duns Scotus on the Will and Morality*, trans. Allan B. Wolter, OFM (Washington, DC: The Catholic University of America Press, 1986), pp. 182–3.
7. *Sed est alia tendentia in potentia eadem ut libera, et active tendat eliciendo actum, ita quod una potentia est duplex tendentia activa et passiva.* Ibid.
8. Scotus, *Ordinatio* lib. IV. d. 49. qq. 9–10.
9. *Sermons and Devotional Writings of Gerard Manley Hopkins*, pp. 174–5.
10. Michael Sylwanowicz, *Contingent Causality and the Foundations of Duns Scotus' Metaphysics* (Leiden: Brill, 1996).
11. See above, Chapter 2.
12. *The Note-Books and Papers of Gerard Manley Hopkins*, p. 344.
13. See above, Chapter 7.
14. *The Note-Books and Papers of Gerard Manley Hopkins*, p. 333.
15. *The Confessions of St. Augustine*, trans. John K. Ryan (New York: Doubleday, 1960), Book 10, Chapter 33.
16. *The Note-Books and Papers of Gerard Manley Hopkins*, p. 98.
17. Gilles Deleuze, *Expressionism in Philosophy: Spinoza*, trans. Martin Joughin (New York: Zone, 1990), chapters 2 and 3. Étienne Gilson, *Jean Duns Scot: Introduction à ses positions fondamentales* (Paris: Vrin, 1952), pp. 248ff.
18. Scotus, *Opus Oxoniense*, lib. I. d. 39. q. 1 n. 13.
19. See above, Chapter 4.

AFTERWORD

1. See above, Chapter 5.
2. *Duns Scotus Metaphysician*, chapter 1. Allan B. Wolter, OFM; *Duns Scotus: Philosophical Writings*, chapter 1.
3. *The Note-Books and Papers of Gerard Manley Hopkins*, p. 332.
4. Chapter 10. See also Chapter 6.

5. See Llewelyn, *The HypoCritical Imagination*.
6. John Ruskin, *The Works of John Ruskin*, vol. iv, p. 251, cited in Lesley Higgins (ed.), *Gerard Manley Hopkins: Oxford Essays and Notes, The Collected Works of Gerard Manley Hopkins*, vol. IV (Oxford: Oxford University Press, 2006), p. 168.
7. Simone Weil, *Gravity and Grace*, trans. Emma Crawford and Mario von der Ruhr (London and New York: Routledge, 1952), p. 32.
8. Ibid. p. 33.
9. Ibid. p. 34.
10. *Summa Theologica*, I: 63, 1–4, *Summa Contra Gentiles*, 3: 110. Miklos Vetö, *The Religious Metaphysics of Simone Weil* (Albany: State University of New York, 1994), p. 176.
11. For what I find myself regarding as an expansion in something like the same spirit as mine, despite its different point of departure, I recommend Elizabeth Templeton's undying *The Strangeness of God* (London: Arthur James, 1993).

Selective Bibliography

JOHN DUNS SCOTUS

I

Balic, C. et al. (eds) (1950–), *Opera Omnia*, Civitas Vaticana: Typis Polyglottis Vaticanis, including *Lectura, Ordinatio* 1–2.3.

Garcia, P. (ed.) (1912), *Commentaria Oxoniensia ad IV. libros magistri Sententiarum*, 2 vols, Quaracchi, Florence: Ad Claras Aquas.

Wadding, L. (ed.) (1968 [1639]), *Opera Omnia*, 12 vols, Lyon: Durand, Hildesheim: Georg Olms Verlagsbuchhandlung, including *Additiones magnae, Questiones super libros Metaphysicorum Aristotelis, Ordinatio (Opus Oxoniense), Questiones quodlibetales, Reportatio Parisiensia, Questiones super praedicamenta Aristotelis*.

II

Bychkov, O. and A. Wolter (eds and trans.) (2004), *Reportatio I-A*, the examined report of the Paris lecture, New York: Saint Bonaventure University, The Franciscan Institute.

Etzkorn, G. and A. Wolter (eds) (1997–8), *Questions on the Metaphysics of Aristotle by John Duns Scotus*, New York: Saint Bonaventure University, The Franciscan Institute.

Frank, W. and A. Wolter (eds and trans.) (1995), *Duns Scotus Metaphysician*, West Lafayette: Purdue University Press.

Garcia, J. (1988), *Introduction to the Problem of Individuation in the Early Middle Ages*, 2nd rev. edn, Munich and Vienna: Philosophia Verlag.

Prentice, R. (1970), *The Basic Quidditative Metaphysics of Duns Scotus as Seen in his De Primo Principio*, Rome: Antonianum.

Sondag, S. (ed. and trans.) (1992), *Le principe d'individuation*, Paris: Vrin.

Spade, P. (ed. and trans.) (1994), *Five Texts on the Mediaeval Problem of Universals*, Indianapolis: Hackett Publishing Company.

Sylwanowicz, M. (1996), *Contingent Causality and the Foundations of Duns Scotus' Metaphysics*, Leiden: Brill.
Wolter, A. (trans.) (1966), *A Treatise on God as First Principle*, Chicago: Franciscan Herald Press.
Wolter, A. (ed. and trans.) (1978), *Duns Scotus: Philosophical Writings*, Indianapolis: Bobbs-Merrill.
Wolter, A. (1986), *Duns Scotus on the Will and Morality*, Washington, DC: The Catholic University of America Press.
Wolter, A. (2005), *Early Oxford Lecture on Individuation*, Latin with English trans., New York: Saint Bonaventure University, The Franciscan Institute.
Wolter, A. and F. Alluntis (eds) (1975), *John Duns Scotus: God and Creatures: The Quodlibetal Questions*, Washington, DC: The Catholic University of America Press.
Wolter, A. and O. Bychkov (eds) (2004), *The Examined Report of the Paris Lecture: Reportatio I-A*, NewYork: Saint Bonaventure University, The Franciscan Institute.

III

Adams, M. (1987), *William Ockham*, 2 vols, Notre Dame: University of Notre Dame Press.
Broadie, A. (1995), *Shadow of Scotus: philosophy and faith in pre-Reformation Scotland*, Edinburgh: T. & T. Clark.
Copleston, F. (1950), *History of Philosophy*, vol. 2, London: Burns Oates and Washbourne.
Cross, R. (1999), *Duns Scotus*, Oxford: Oxford University Press.
Gilson, É. (1952), *Jean Duns Scot: Introduction à ses positions fondamentales*, Paris: Vrin.
Harris, C. (1927), *Duns Scotus*, 2 vols, Oxford: Clarendon Press.
Heidegger, M. (1916), *Die Kategorien- und Bedeutungslehre des Duns Scotus*, Tübingen: Mohr.
Heidegger, M. (1970), *Traité des catégories et de la signification chez Duns Scotus*, trans. Florent Gaboriau, Paris: Gallimard.
Heidegger, M. (1978), *Frühe Schriften, Gesamtausgabe* 1, ed. Friedrich-Wilhelm von Hermann, Frankfurt am Main: Klostermann.
Honnefelder, L. R. Wood and M. Dreyer (eds) (1996), *John Duns Scotus: Metaphysics and Ethics*, Leiden: Brill.
Ingham, M. and M. Dreyer (2004), *The Philosophical Vision of John Duns Scotus: An Introduction*, Washington, DC: The Catholic University of America.
Leff, G. (1975), *William of Ockham: The Metamorphosis of Scholastic Discourse*, Manchester: Manchester University Press.
Ryan, J. and B. Bonansea (eds) (1965), *John Duns Scotus, 1265–1965*, Washington, DC: The Catholic University of America.
Shircel, C. (1942), *The Univocity of the Concept of Being in the Philosophy of John Duns Scotus*, Washington, DC: The Catholic University of America.
Vos, A. et al. (2003), *Duns Scotus on Divine Love: Texts and Commentary on Goodness and Freedom, God and Humans*, Aldershot: Ashgate.

Selective Bibliography

Williams T. (ed.) (2002), *The Cambridge Companion to Duns Scotus*, Cambridge: Cambridge University Press.
Wolter, A. (1946), *The Transcendentals and their Function in the Metaphysics of Duns Scotus*, New York: Saint Bonaventure University, The Franciscan Institute.

GERARD MANLEY HOPKINS

I

Abbott, C. (ed.) (1955), *The Correspondence of Gerard Manley Hopkins and Richard Watson Dixon*, London: Oxford University Press.
Abbott, C. (ed.) (1955), *The Letters of Gerard Manley Hopkins to Robert Bridges*, London: Oxford University Press.
Abbott, C. (ed.) (1957), *Further Letters of Gerard Manley Hopkins, Including his Correspondence with Coventry Patmore*, London: Oxford University Press.
Devlin, C. (ed.) (1959), *Sermons and Devotional Writings of Gerard Manley Hopkins*, London: Oxford University Press.
Gardner, W. (ed.) (1963), *Poems and Prose of Gerard Manley Hopkins*, London: Penguin.
Higgins, L. (ed.) (2006), *Oxford Essays and Notes, The Collected Works of Gerard Manley Hopkins*, vol. IV, Oxford: Oxford University Press.
House, H. (ed.) (1937), *The Note-Books and Papers of Gerard Manley Hopkins*, London: Oxford University Press.
House, H. and G. Storey (eds) (1959), *The Journals and Papers of Gerard Manley Hopkins*, Oxford: Oxford University Press.
Mackenzie, N. (ed.) (1990), *The Poetical Works of Gerard Manley Hopkins*, Oxford: Clarendon Press.
Thornton, R. and C. Phillips (eds) (2013), *The Collected Works of Gerard Manley Hopkins*, vols I–II: *Correspondence*, Oxford: Oxford University Press.

II

Gardner, W. (1966), *Gerard Manley Hopkins: A Study of Poetic Idiosyncrasy in Relation to Poetic Tradition*, 2 vols, London: Oxford University Press.
Hartman, G. (ed.) (1966), *Hopkins: A Collection of Critical Essays*, Englewood Cliffs, NJ: Prentice-Hall.
MacKenzie, N. (1981), *A Reader's Guide to Gerard Manley Hopkins*, London: Thames and Hudson.
Miller, J. (1963), *The Disappearance of God*, Cambridge, MA: Harvard University Press.
Pick, J. (1966), *Gerard Manley Hopkins: Priest and Poet*, London: Oxford University Press.
Roberts, G. (1994), *Gerard Manley Hopkins: A Literary Life*, London: Macmillan.
Weyand, N. (ed.) (1949), *Immortal Diamond: Studies in Gerard Manley Hopkins*, London: Sheed and Ward.
White, N. (1998), *Gerard Manley Hopkins in Wales*, Bridgend: Seren.

Index

abduction, 79
Abel, K., 4, 45
address, 39, 91, 94, 123
   existence, 90–1
aesthethics, 6, 56, 84, 89, 121, 122, 128
   aesthethical turn, 60
   affection, 122
agapology, 115
   agathology, 117
agnotology, 109
Alexander of Hales, 48
Alféri, P., 92–3
Anselm, Saint, ontological argument, 91, 118, 130
Antisthenes, 16
Aquinas, Saint Thomas, 14, 15, 91
   analogicality of being, 96
   attention deficit disorder, 131
Arendt, H., Heidegger, M., 117–19
Aristotle
   analogicality of being, 96
   Metaphysics, 20, 30, 62
   poēma, 56
   praxis, 56
Armstrong, D., 101, 106, 107
as-if, 8, 75, 78
   if-then, 79, 122, 128
attention, 4, 7, 14, 100
   intention, 4, 117, 121–2
   waiting (*attendre*), 122
   willing not to will, 120
attentionality and intentionality, 89, 131

attestation, 5
Augustine, Saint, 14, 32, 46, 118
   intuited truths, 98
   quaestio mihi, 123
Austin, J.
   the beautiful, 54
   linguistic phenomenology, 44
   performativity, 34
Averrhoes, 25, 51, 101
Avicenna
   horseness, 24, 34, 36, 47, 76
   intentio formalis, 40

Baker, J., 65, 70, 83, 86
barbarisms, 6, 26, 27, 35, 39, 86
Barnes, W., 12
beauty, 24, 48, 54
   Cinderella Transcendental, 128
   expression, 55–6
   love, 59
   rhyme, 20
   Scotus, J., 64
behaviour, 24–5
Being, 19, 21, 48–9
Burnet, J., 19, 107
   doing, 26, 27, 34, 35, 78, 99–107
   God, 22
   letting-be, 120
   the one, 22
   seeming, 72, 74
   univocality, 49, 96
Boler, J., 83
Bridges, R., 23, 30, 61
Butler, J., identity, 48

categoricality, absolute, 94
categories, 47–50
chiasm, 6, 7, 28, 35
  of intention and attention, 123
Christ, 14, 63, 128
Collingwood, R., 111–13
common natures, 8, 36–9, 41, 47, 71, 103, 124
constatement, performativity, 91, 94, 98, 113
contraction, 10, 21, 24, 27, 36, 40, 46–7, 95
  two kinds, 96
creation, 12–13, 17, 31, 58–9, 128
  decreation, 130
  ex nihilo, 114
  praise, 75, 102
crux, 105
cynghanedd, 24–5

Dawkins, R., 76
death, 52, 123
decreation, 32, 130
Deleuze, G.
  attributes and properties, 125
  immanence, 125
  Spinoza, B., 125
Derrida, J., 93, 94
  performativity, 34
Descartes, R., 31–2
design, 58, 79, 128
destruction, 106
Devlin, C., 59, 128
disponibility, 129
Duffy, C., the verb dancing at the heart of the noun, 78

emphatically definite descriptions, 39–40, 85, 120, 128
ens and *entitas*, 33–4, 48, 125
equiprimordiality, 15, 51
ergontology, 14
essence, existence, 91–2
existence, 13, 43–4, 81, 91–2, 106
  essence, 91–2
  the ex (from) of existence, 83, 88
  and goodness, 42, 53, 108, 118, 131
  Hume, D., 92
experimentum suitatis, 4

fact and fate, 26, 28, 52
faculties of mind, 42
Firstness, Secondness and Thirdness in Peirce, 80–1, 83–4
foredrawing, 20, 22, 45

forepitch, 122
formal distinction (*distinctio formalis*), 4, 8, 29, 36–7, 41, 60, 90, 105
  and *haecceitas*, 42, 47, 58, 91
  of inscape and instress, 52
  of intention and attention, 7, 53
  praxis and *poiesis*, 65
  and the synthetic a priori, 98
freedom of will, 53, 129, 130
Frege, G., 34, 49

Giles of Rome, 38, 108
God, 42, 57, 58, 76
  if there be any, 108
  love, 115, 124
Godfrey of Fontaines, 104
goodness, 29, 46, 50, 53, 55, 89, 90, 124
  and existence, 53, 108
  Plato, 116
grace, 62, 63
Grote, J., 49, 69, 110

habit, 80, 82
haecceity (*haecceitas*, thisness), 7, 8, 13, 21, 28, 32, 33, 34, 35, 36, 78
  and *distinctio formalis*, 42
  ecceitas, 94
  Leibniz, G., 57
  proximity (*Nähe*), 46
Hegel, G., 18, 20, 30, 45, 51
Peirce, C., 83
Heidegger, M., 18, 45
  Arendt, H., 118
  Befindlichkeit, 46
Henry of Ghent, 15, 37, 96, 100
Heraclitus, 24
Herbert, G., 61–2, 115–16
horseness, 34, 36, 47, 76
Hume, D., existence, 92
Husserl, E., 44–5

if-then, 8, 78, 79
  as-if, 122, 128
  ex-istence, 84
Ignatius Loyola, Saint, 12–13, 26, 32, 102, 120
ignorance, nominal and verbal, 109–10
imadgination, 86–7
imagination, 8, 93, 128–9
  adverbiality, 75
Incarnation, 18, 58, 128
indication *see* pointing
individuality, 86
  existence, 42

148

ground of, 10, 38, 42, 89, 95, 108, 114
particularity, 20, 21, 32, 34, 36–9, 41, 124
inscape, 9, 10, 13, 16, 128
Bridges, R., 22–3
schaffen, 12
instress, 9, 10, 13
running, 10–11, 24, 41
will, 63
intentio formalis, 40
intention, 7, 14
and attention, 117, 121–2
intentionality, 49, 122
and attentionality, 89, 131
first and second, 34, 92

Jemeinigkeit, 51, 93
jizz, 70, 72
Job, 5, 16
justices, 63, 95, 114, 120
universal and singular, 96

Kant, I., 60
existence, 85
first and third *Critique*, 70
schematism, 128
Keats, J., 56

landscape, 25
Leibniz, G.
identity of indiscernibles, 57
petites perceptions, 14
truths of reason and of fact, 96
Levinas, E., 109
justices and equality, 95
love, 115
'reversal', 121
likeness, 8, 33, 56, 71, 73, 83, 86, 128
difference and diversity, 57
family, 44–5
identity, 11
listen, 56, 91
Locke, J., power includes relation, 80
look, 34, 56, 91, 94
Wittgenstein, L., 17
love, 6, 8, 53
amo: volo ut sis, 8, 118
beauty, 59
Herbert, G., 61–2, 115–16
Levinas, E., 115
loveliness, 60–1, 121
of wisdom and wisdom of love (sophophily), 52, 130–1

middle voice, 5, 113–14, 120, 123, 129
Miller, J. Hillis, rhyme, 20
Mourelatos, A., veridical 'is', 26, 48–9
Muybridge, E., 24
myth, 129

near-tautology, 98
Nicholas of Cusa, 109
Nominalism and Scholastic realism, 81, 87

Ockham, W., 81–2, 92–3
offscape, 15
Olivi, J., 4
outscape, 14
outstress, 14

Parmenides, 9, 11, 18–27, 41, 48, 50, 73, 99, 131
particularity, 36, 104
singularity, 124
Passmore, J., the dreariness of aesthetics, 54
Pater, W., music, 58
pattern, 58, 79, 128
peculiarity, 70, 95, 103
Peirce, C., 79
Firstness, Secondness and Thirdness in Peirce, 80–1, 83–4
index, icon, symbol, 88
perfection, 53
performativity, 34–5, 52
constatement, 91, 94, 98, 113
personality, 13, 15, 22, 25, 28, 42, 52, 69, 70, 107
philosophy, Hopkins, 130
pitch, 15, 17, 28, 31–3, 78
stress, 94
Plato, 22
pointing, 88–9, 91, 100, 121
Potter, D., 16–17, 71, 103, 106, 120
practice, primacy of, 50, 80
pragmatism and pragmaticism, 79, 82
predication, 90
existence, 91
presuppositions, 111–13, 115, 117
Pythagoras, 24

quaintance, 49, 69, 86, 97

Ramsey, F., singing and whistling, 35
recipience, 123
regard, 123

Reid, T., 86–7
  principles of common sense, 98
religious, the, 7, 9, 22, 60, 75, 109, 124, 127, 130
res, 64
Rodin, A., 17, 22
Ruskin, J., 10, 60, 129
Russell, B., 69, 110
  knowledge by acquaintance and description, 49

sake, 11–12, 15, 56, 84, 124
science, 31, 71, 78
  scientia, 20, 44, 76, 92, 105
seeming, being, 72, 74
self-taste, 5, 51, 59, 77
shudder-quotes, 6, 15, 25
  Goethe's Faust, 6, 125, 130
signification, 45, 49–50, 82, 88
singing, 35
singularity *see* individuality
solitude (*Einsamkeit*), 93, 97
Spinoza, B., 125
sprung rhythm, 24
strangeness, 4, 30, 35, 39, 70, 86, 103, 131
sublimity, 55, 60, 121, 123, 124, 130
suchness, 34
sufficient reason, principle of, 31–2

Thomas, D., 4
Thomas, E., 44, 58
Thomas of Erfurt, 34, 45
transcendens, 48
transcendentals, 50, 54
Trinity, 42, 63, 91, 101
Turner, J., 10, 23, 44

unity, less than numerical, 36, 47
universals, 39, 47
univocality, 38, 49, 96
unravelling, 3–4

vocation, 105, 123 (*Aufgabe*, calling)

waiting, 122
Weil, S.
  attention, 131
  decreation, 130–1
will, 8, 28
  affective and active, 64, 119
  attention, 120
  freedom, 25, 28, 53, 129
  instress, 63
  intellect, 41, 91, 117
  passive and active, 14, 119
  pitch, 28
  primacy of, 15, 28, 117
  suffering, 75
  volo ut sis, 8, 118
  wanting, 118–19
  will not to will, 8, 87, 119–21, 124
wisdom, of love and love of wisdom, 52, 130–1
Wittgenstein, L.
  address, 39
  detached colour-impression, 39
  family resemblance, 44–5
  look, 17, 44
world, 90
  edge of, 76–7

yes and *is*, 19, 22, 26, 94, 99–100, 123
  Amen, 123

EU representative:
Easy Access System Europe
Mustamäe tee 50, 10621 Tallinn, Estonia
Gpsr.requests@easproject.com

www.ingramcontent.com/pod-product-compliance
Lightning Source LLC
Chambersburg PA
CBHW071849230426
43671CB00012B/2120